MW00628362

WORDS

NO KETCHUP

"Keep this book in your car and you'll never be more than ten minutes away from finding a great city hot dog joint. How about an all-suburban edition next?!"

–Bob Sirott, WGN Radio

"The Streets and San Man writes again, and he hasn't lost his snap. It takes a real tube steak to write the definitive book on Chicago's best hot dogs, and Dennis Foley is pure beef with a healthy splash of mustard."

–Mark Brown, *Chicago Sun-Times*

No Ketchup is like a picnic on Chicago's lakefront on a warm day, like a seat in the bleachers at Wrigley (yes, Wrigley) Field for a double header in the sunshine, like the smell of French fries and a properly snappy dog in a grease-spotted bag next to you as you drive up Clark Street with your windows open to the breezes and WXRT blasting from the radio. This, Dennis Foley's most recent love letter to Chicago, will leave you both hungry and satisfied, and eager to try every one of these hot dog joints and the delicacies they offer. Chicago's history of hard work and tenacity and the pursuit of happiness by way of the hotdog is told by the proprietors of these meat-based meccas, and Foley collects their stories and serves them up hot and with everything (except ketchup!)

–Patricia Ann McNair, author of *And These Are The Good Times,* and *The Temple of Air*

"*No Ketchup* has all the ingredients of a Chicago-style read: Plenty of fun, no skimping on the info, a hefty helping of hot dog history and full of snap."

–Grace Kuikman, *The Villager*

PRAISE for
THE STREETS AND SAN MAN'S GUIDE TO CHICAGO EATS

"The former electrician for the city's Department of Streets and Sanitation has become a local icon since releasing *The Streets and San Man's Guide to Chicago Eats.*"

–Robert Elfinger, *Chicago Tribune*

"The book is based on a simple premise: Who better to advise you on where to grab a tasty, afford-able midday meal in Chicago's neighborhoods than people who consider lunch to be the highlight of the work day? You always assumed this was true, but Foley confirms it in enough detail that, tongue-in-cheek or not, you will be more than tempted to take his dining tips."

–Mark Brown, *Chicago Sun-Times*

"As soon as *The Streets and San Man's Guide to Chicago Eats* hit our desk, we went out and tried a couple of author Dennis Foley's picks. Boy were they good! Foley's choices are mostly no-nonsense places that emphasize hearty servings at great prices, often in neighborhoods the critics never hit."

–*Chicago Sun-Times*, Food

Also by Dennis Foley:

THE BLUE CIRCUS (Side Street Press, 2018)

THE DRUNKARD'S SON (Side Street Press, 2012)

THE STREETS AND SAN MAN'S GUIDE TO CHICAGO EATS
(Lake Claremont Press, 2004)

NOT A STRANGER, a film (Uncork'd Entertainment, 2018 –
available on Amazon Prime)

No Ketchup

Chicago's Top 50 Hot Dogs
and
The Stories Behind Them

Dennis Foley

A McBRIDE AND ROCHE PRESS BOOK

Published by
McBride and Roche Press
Chicago, Illinois

McRO
PRESS

formerly Side Street Press
www.mcropress.com

Copyright: Dennis Foley, 2020

All rights reserved. No part of this book may be reproduced or transmitted in any form or by any means, electronic or mechanical, including photocopying, recording, or by any information storage or retrieval system without written permission from the publisher, except for the inclusion of brief quotations in a review or where permitted by law.

ISBN: 978-0-9988039-3-7

Printed in the United States of America

First Edition: September, 2020

Cover by Patrick Foley

For all those who hold the Chicago Hot Dog as near and dear to their hearts as I do. To my buddy Paulie Serritella: thanks for coming up with the title for this tome. And to Everett Foley, my new grandson and heir to the Foley throne: may you enjoy many Chicago dogs in your day.

Table of Contents

A note on the structure in this book: there is none. I'm a big-time believer in letting the potato chips—or in this case, hot dogs—fall where they may. To find a specific hot dog stand, check out the Location Guide in the Index (Pages 117-121).

Introduction

So here're the facts—plain and simple. I know food.
And I most certainly know hot dogs. See, I did a little
work in my first life as an electrician with the City of
Chicago's Department of Streets and San. And sure, I did
some work each day, but mostly I drove the streets of our
fair city in a baby blue van in search of mom and pop
eateries where you could get some outstanding chow at a
reasonable price. Nice gig, huh? And within that
wonderful world of local food hails one of our city's
greatest creations—the Chicago style hot dog. First

introduced to the public in 1893 at the Chicago World's Fair (Columbian Exhibition), the Chicago dog has become part of the fabric of a local's life. Ah yes, the Chicago dog—fit for kings, queens, and commoners alike.

During my seven year stretch with Streets and San, I visited virtually every top-notch dog stand in the city. We worked, and we ate lunch. That's how the job went. And just recently I set out on a new mission: **50 Hot Dogs in 50 Days**. Can you say, Yummy? My wife gave me a bewildered wag of her head when I shared my idea, and then she immediately put in a call to up the amount on my life insurance policy. Well, I ended up eating far more than 50 dogs in those 50 days but here in this book you will find my Top 50 Chicago hot dogs (plus a few extras), as well as some stories about the folks behind the dog—the owners who slap the mustard on those tasty wieners.

This brings me to the all-important question: So what makes a great Chicago hot dog? No doubt, the answer to this formidable question could be debated for hours upon end by the players at City Hall. And the search for that answer could lead to citywide fistfights among hot dog fanatics claiming that the dog served at their neighborhood stand is, in fact, the city's best. That being said, in my humble opinion, here are a few things that go into making a great Chicago dog.

1. Above and beyond all else—I'm an all-beef-or-nothing hot dog guy. I already eat enough bacon and sausage annually to support several Iowa pig farmers, so when it comes to hot dogs, I say, BRING ON THE BEEF.

2. And quite frankly, a quality dog must look the part and have some giddy up to it. C'mon, you know what

I'm talking about here, right? You can see that slight curve to the dog when it rests in your bun and feel that SNAP when you sink your teeth into its skin.

3. Next, the dog should be steamed to perfection (though I am learning to enjoy a good char dog). The bun: I prefer poppy seed but have no problem with a plain bun. But no matter what–the bun must be steamed. No exceptions. None. None. None.

4. And then there are the extras that get tossed on top of the dog. I like to call these ingredients, **The Magnificent Seven**. No, I'm not talking about the old 1960 Western starring the likes of Yul Brynner, Steve McQueen (my man) and Charles Bronson (can you say, *Death Wish*?). No, I'm talking about the following dog toppings:

1. Mustard
2. Onions
3. Relish
4. Tomatoes
5. Pickle (cucumber is an acceptable substitute, or both)
6. Sport peppers
7. Celery salt

*And by the way . . . don't even try to tell me that the 2016 remake of *The Magnificent Seven*, starring Denzel Washington, was better than the original. Sure I love Denzel, but there's no chance. None. None. None.

Now these ingredients must be fresh and bountiful. We all know when the owner of a dog joint is skimping on the extras. Maybe the tomatoes were around when your grandmother was born, or perhaps the dill pickle has a side job as a stunt double for a toothpick. In short, if a dog joint skimps on the ingredients or doesn't offer the entire Magnificent Seven selection, or if it fails to steam the buns, then that place is essentially dead to me. And hey, dog slingers, while it's not a deal breaker, don't go forgettin' the celery salt. C'mon, that last little pinch of dust adds just the oomph needed to make this a creation that would have been suitable for the Last Supper.

5. What else? Well, beyond the dog itself, there's something about a quality hot dog stand that just gives off a good feel and makes eating a dog a pleasurable experience. Maybe it's the mom or pop owner hustling behind the counter and offering a toothy grin as he or she slips that dog into its bun. Maybe it's because while you're standing in line or munching on your dog at the window counter, you can hear the owner recite from memory the orders of the regulars when they walk through the door. *"Hey, Jimmy Boy, good to see ya. You want the regular—two dogs with everything, easy on the mustard, easy on the onions, with a fry and a Coke?"* Service like that is priceless. And sure, while I like good service, I'm not looking for some kiss-ass, plastic mannequin who's gonna Yes-Sir me to death as I order my food. No, I want service from real Chicagoans, from folks who like to use a few dis, dat, dese and doses, from folks who aren't afraid to tell some patron to bug off when he's acting like a clown. And maybe it's because the helper busting his ass working the stove for twelve hours a day is new to our country and places like these help put some coin in his pocket so he has a chance to begin his new life.

6. And there's something to be said about the way the exterior of a top-notch hot dog stand looks. They don't have to be pieces of art but like a good character actor,

there's something about them that simply stands out. Maybe it's the sign swinging with the wind above the door, or the dancing mascot on the roof, or the bright colors that invite you to a feeling of yesteryear.

Don's drive In – 78th and Kedzie

In short, a great Chicago hot dog carries a piece of all these items. I'm sure I could toss a few more things out there about the makings of a great Chicago dog, and I have no doubt you could throw a few ideas my way, as well. But I'll stop here for now before I turn this thing into a novel.

Ratings

All of the Chicago Hot Dogs in this book have received one of the following ratings:

Excellent

Very Good

Good

*If you would like a hot dog that falls below 3 stars, there are plenty out there. Believe me. I've eaten dogs that could double as a rubber hose, been served a dog warmed up in a microwave (should be a felony), and had dogs that just simply weren't all that tasty. Maybe some clueless clown would be okay with dogs like that, but not me. You won't find any of those ragtag dog joints in this book. Why? My goal was not to rip on a place with a sorry-ass dog or on a place that skimps, but rather to give you a pocket book suitable for tossing in your glove box where you could get a quick reference for a quality hot dog stand wherever you might happen to be in the city.

Terms

M7 – The Magnificent 7 ingredients
Thummy – A hot dog as thick as your thumb
Pinky – a hot dog as thick as your pinky finger

Prices

Most hot dogs in this book range from \$2.50-3.99. Some come with mandatory fries and the prices jump a bit then. You will find a few specialty dogs priced in the \$5-10 range, but those are a rarity. Overall, at an average of roughly \$3.00, the Chicago hot dog remains a great blue-collar steak. But please know this: Not all wieners are created equal. Perhaps, an old girlfriend has already mentioned this to you. In the Chicago Hot Dog world, our royalty is as follows: Vienna Beef (the undisputed King) and the underlings (princes)—David Berg and Red Hot Chicago. But even within the Vienna Beef hot dog world, for example, there are skinless dogs, and encased dogs (which most folks, myself included, think of when discussing a Chicago dog with snap). And then there's the size factor. Even within the Vienna family, some dogs are skinnier than others. To put this in true layman's terms—some dogs are like your pinky (a Pinky) and some like your thumb (a Thummy). So just because one dog joint is selling a dog for \$2.25 and another for \$3.25, don't assume that the guy with the more expensive dog is a thankless thief. Just remember—size does matter.

The Lowdown

Sadly, mom and pop businesses are a dying breed, not just here in Chicago, but everywhere you cast your eyes. And Covid 19 certainly didn't help matters. But in this book, we get to hear from some of these mom and pop owners while they're still around to breathe life into their stories as well as make their great dogs. I hope you enjoy the ride.

Jake's Pup in the Ruf
4401 N Sheridan, Chicago
773-728-1188   Rating:

Sure this Uptown fixture now serves just about everything under the sun (opens at 5:30 AM so get your hearty breakfast egg sandwich here), but there's no denying Jake's roots as a hot dog joint. This place has been kicking out dogs since 1959, and the dog they currently pump out ($2.99) is still A-1 quality. This Thummy carries all of the M7 ingredients including a full Frisbee-sized slice of tomato set atop the whole shebang. Niiiiice. Give the broasted chicken ($5.99 for 2 legs and 2 thighs) a try sometime if you're not feeling a dog. Damn tasty for sure.

A Vienna Beef Hall of Famer since 2006, Jake's has also helped many Uptown homeless over the years in need of a meal. If you dine in, grab a seat near the back so you can sit beside "The Hot Dog Field of Dreams Dog." I don't know what the owners call it, but that's what I call it. This five-foot hot dog is snoozed out on a blue fiberglass couch, and he's having a dream where he's standing at home plate about to hit a long ball. Maybe the Cubbies will have him in centerfield this year.

Kimski

960 W 31st Street, Chicago

773-823-7336   Rating:

Sign me up as a fan of the KoPo experience. The Polish with fries ($8.99) comes loaded with spicy mustard, scallions, sesame seeds, a fermented purple cabbage kraut, and kimchi hot sauce on a bread bun. To get this fusion of Korean and Polish foods, you'll need to roll into Bridgeport where owner Mike Marszewski is the mastermind behind this cultural marriage made in heaven. The wings are spicy and rock solid ($12.00) and the dressed fries ($7.00) are otherworldly. I hit this place on a Sunday at noon, right after they opened. If you like it quiet, sit up front by the window overlooking 31st Street. If you want to check out the vibe inside, it's worth it. The music will be jamming and the bevvies will be flowing.

Around the corner

The **Bridgeport Art Center** (at Racine and 35th Street) is just a few blocks away. Pop in and check it out. Feel the need for a cold craft beer and a brewery with a cool vibe? **Marz Community Brewing Company** (3630 S Iron, Chicago), owned by Ed Marszewski (those Marszewski boys, they're such busy guys) fills both requirements. For a perfect Sunday: Skip church and head to Kimski at noon for a Polish, some dressed fries, and a beer, and then head to Marz for another brew. With 24 beers on tap, you'll find plenty to like.

Fat Tommy's

3031 W 111th Street, Chicago

773-233-3287   Rating:

Fat Tommy's offers a top-notch Chicago dog ($3) just the way I like it with all of the M7s, including a cucumber slice in place of the dill pickle (that's right up my alley). The condiments are fresh and the dog has plenty of snap. If you don't mind loosening your belt a notch, Nikki Johnson, one of the Fat Tommy cooks, suggests their Polish sausage wrapped in bacon and then deep fried. Doesn't that sound just wonderful? After it comes out of the fryer, they slide it into a bun and top it with mustard, grilled onions and cheese. It's called the Ditka ($5.50), in honor of the almighty and all-powerful coach (Matt Nagy has a lot of work ahead of him before he gets a sausage named in his honor). And if chili is your game, tell Nikki to throw some on top of the Ditka. At that point, it transforms into—The Butkus ($5.85). Ah yes, that's my kind of sandwich.

If you're feeling burger-ish, I suggest the Brie-oche Bacon Burger (a hand-packed burger on a brioche bun, served with brie cheese and a smidge of apricot jam for $10.50) which includes a side of fresh cut fries. You can thank me later. And hey, let's not forget the beer (and how could we?). Fat Tommy's picked up its liquor license several years ago, so if you feel the need to swill a quality bevy or two or three with your chow of choice, you can have at it.

The Lowdown

Fat Tommy's - Five Minutes of Happiness

It's never a good thing when you take a painful tumble down a Wisconsin ski slope and end up with two broken thumbs, pins inserted into the thumb bones, and surgery. That's a major double ouch. But when that 1991 incident led then twenty-five-year-old Dan Coogan to shift careers and get into the hot dog game, I guess you could say that tumble down that snowy slope and the two plaster trophies that followed were well worth it.

"I had two arm casts for three months. I couldn't work," says Dan, the owner of Fat Tommy's. "So I came up with the idea of opening a hot dog cart. And I told my friend Tom Braekey about it. He was tired of his print industry job and he wanted in."

Tom tossed $1200 into the mix. Dan reached into his own pockets and came up with two nickels. So he did what any young, would-be entrepreneur with two nickels to his name would do—he hit up his parents for a $1200 loan. Thank God for moms and dads. The result: D&T's Cart in the Park kicked into gear in 1991 with its home base at Kennedy Park at 113th and Western. After nine years of working the cart at the park, Dan and Tom opened their first store on 111th Street in Mt. Greenwood.

"That place had some good food history to it," Dan says. "Just before us, the Dog House was there. And back in the '50s, Wonderburger (a Mt. Greenwood staple for over half a century) was there. And in the '70s some guy named Vic cooked burgers in there and wrapped them in newspaper." Ah yes, the good old days, when Chicago newspapers were plentiful and glad to find a second life as hamburger wrap.

Not long after the move, Dan bought out Tom and in 2009 moved the business down the street to its current location on the corner of 111th and Whipple, just a stone's throw east of Kedzie.

Dan Coogan

Several booths and a number of tables dot the floor. The rest of the seating area is decked out with posters, sports paraphernalia, photos of other dog joints, a half-wall shrine of obituary mass cards, a record player and a sizeable stack of records—for customers in the mood for some tunage while they munch. One sign on the west wall catches my interest. It's touted as the BASEBALL SPECIAL. A devout Sox fan, Dan has no love or use for the team in blue from the other side of town, and this sign makes it abundantly clear. When I ask Dan about the sign, he snatches it from the wall and reads it proudly to me: "If the Sox win and the Cubs lose, the next day between 2:00pm and 5:00pm, Hot dogs are $1.50."

Ouch again. As a South Side Cubs fan, I don't like to see the Cubs lose on any day. But if they happen to lose and the Sox just so happen to win, if I can get a great dog at a 1990s price, I'm good with the way the world works.

Dan sets the sign back in place and takes on a different tone. "I don't think I would still be in this business if it wasn't for my wife, Caroline." I ask if Caroline works at Fat Tommy's. "No. She works in the marketing department for Benjamin Moore. With me here and her there, it's like the separation of church and state." He smiles. "But she's the backbone of the business. And her marketing background has been a huge help. For instance, take the kitchen sink salad on the menu (the In A Gadda da Vida, named after the 1968 Iron Butterfly song). My wife designed it and wanted me to put it on the menu but I was against it. She said she used to make the salad in college and everyone thought it was delicious. I figured I'd sell one per week and it would be to her. Well, I was dead wrong. Later that week I called home and apologized. The salad was a huge hit. People here love that salad ($7.00), especially when you add Cajun chicken and a raspberry vinaigrette ($10.50). It's a big seller on our menu now."

A hard-working man who regularly puts in 12-hour days, Dan has an easy way about him, an authentic way. Regulars march in and out of the place, exchange barbs with Dan, grab food orders, shake hands and head out on their way. Other regulars come in and sit at a table after they order. And new faces come in, too. All are welcome and Dan treats them all the same.

"Everyone deserves five minutes of happiness," Dan says. "When some people come in here, they want to eat and talk and have fun. Others want to grab a newspaper and sit and read while they eat. I just want them to be happy. And giving them a good meal and treating them right can do that. This is a family place too. People have been coming to Fat Tommy's for a long time. Now they bring their kids in with them."

If you wanted to get a true feel for Mt. Greenwood, you could stroll up and down 111th street near Kedzie and check out some shops, pubs and eateries, perhaps take a walk past the nearby firehouse, or you could just push through the side door to Fat Tommy's, take a seat in a booth, and Mt. Greenwood's heart and soul would come to you–courtesy of Dan Coogan.

Wolfy's Hot Dogs
2734 W Peterson, Chicago
773-743-0207

Rating:

One of my GO TO dog spots for over 20 years, Wolfy's is a West Rogers Park treasure. Sure I'm drawn to the gigantic fork and dog outside this place (Who wouldn't be?), but the dog itself ($2.69 and a Thummy) is downright fantastic. It carries all of the M7s and never fails to bark with its big-time snap. If I did a blind taste test, I could always pick out this dog. The fresh ingredients, the snap–it's that damn good. The Polish with mustard, grilled onion, tomatoes and pickle ($4.09) is also a keeper. A Vienna Beef Hall of Famer, there's a reason Wolfy's has been around since 1967. This dog is primo and a contender for Top Dog in the city.

35th Street Red Hots
500 W 35th Street, Chicago
773-823-7336   Rating:

This place comes at you with a nice dog (a Pinky) and fresh cut fries on top of the dog for $3.62. There is no M7 here. Rather, the dog is covered with mustard, relish, onions, and sport peppers. Sure I like this dog, and the fresh cut fries are always good, but the shrimp here is out-damn-standing. A half-pound of prawns will run you about $9 and double it for the full pound. This place is tied in with the Wiener Circle and Red Hot Ranch. While I give the dog 3.5 mustards, the shrimp gets 4. A great stop before or after a White Sox game.

Susie's Drive Thru
4126 W Montrose, Chicago
773-283-6544   Rating:

Like Fat Johnnies on the South Side, Susie's is a

definite dog "shack," with fervent followers who go back decades. This place screams old school and kicks out a solid dog ($3.18) or with excellent fresh cut fries ($4.31). This Pinky comes with all the M7 fixings and tosses a cucumber wedge into the mix for fun. The folks at Alderman Samantha Nugent's office (Ward 39) suggested Susie's when I checked in with them. If you wanna know where some good greasy spoons are in any area, check in with the alderman. They know their turf.

If you're the type of person who likes to knock down a beast bowl at almost any hour, I highly recommend the cheese fries in a humongozoid edible tortilla bowl—a bargain at $6.89, or check out the Confused Chicken sandwich ($9.32), a foot-long, game changer served with fresh veggies and Italian and Greek spices. Voted one of *Chicago's Best* drive thrus, Susie's is a must.

The Low Down
Susie's Drive Thru – All in the Family

Not long after little Susie Karda waltzed into the world in the early '70s, her parents—Gus and Kathy Ninos—named their new eatery in her honor, and thus Susie's Drive Thru was also born. Perhaps you would think Susie's older sister, Stacy, might be a wee bit jealous of these naming rights. But such was not the case. Back then, Stacy already had a diner named after her.

"My parents had a couple of different places over the years," says Susie. "'Stacy's' was a diner over on Belmont near Kostner. But my parents eventually just focused on this place. It was originally the Western

Burger when my dad bought it, but he changed the name just a few months after I was born."

A staple in the Irving Park neighborhood for 45 years, Susie, Stacy, and Laura Migon (Susie's mother-in-law) now run the Susie show.

Susie's Drive Thru

"I first started working here when I was around eleven or twelve. My mom used to bring me in with her on Saturdays." Susie laughs. "I used to do the little things back then. Handle the drinks, put the fries in the fryer. Things like that."

When she was fourteen, Susie started working full-time at her namesake during the summers. It was then that she observed her father's way of handling the restaurant.

"My dad had a system for everything in the restaurant. He had a system for cooking the perfect hot dog, a system for getting the oil just right for the French fries. How to organize food in the cooler. He had a system for things like that and more."

It was Susie's mother, though, who in the '80s came up with one of my favorite culinary concoctions–the Confused Chicken sandwich, a foot-long whopper.

"My mom used to put Greek seasonings and Italian seasonings and some other seasonings on that sandwich. And then she'd add the peppers and veggies and joke that, 'This chicken doesn't know if it's Greek or Italian or something else. It's definitely confused.'"

I am a man humbled by this tasty behemoth of a sandwich. It's a perfect melting pot of spices, chicken, peppers, onions, cheese and bread. It has become one of my new favorite big sandwiches, right there with my old staple–the Italian sub from Bari Foods. So to you, Kathy Ninos, I say, THANK YOU from the bottom of my satisfied stomach.

Gus passed away in 2008 and Kathy in 2016. But they are both here in spirit. "They worked hard to make this place a success," says Susie. "A place where people can get quality food."

In the early days, the drive thru focused on hot dogs, Polish sausages, the Super taco, and milk shakes. Over the years, the menu expanded, in large part to meet the demands of its old 24-hour schedule (now open 9AM to roughly 11PM/later on the weekend). "But recently, we removed some items from the menu," Susie says. "We kept our favorites and then added some new items. I felt it was time for some changes."

In addition to the dog and the Confused Chicken sandwich, other popular items are their milkshakes, Philly cheese, and cheese fries. "People really like our cheese fries in the tortilla bowl," Susie says. "Some just get cheese. Others get chili with it. It's a big item on the menu."

One of the new items on the menu, added as the Midway Monsters were about to kickoff the season, is the Bears Special—a large croissant stuffed with Italian Beef and smothered in liquid cheddar cheese. "People love that sandwich," Susie says "so we're leaving it on the menu even though the Bears season is over."

Ah yes, Susie, thanks for that sad reminder. The Bears season is definitely over. As I write these words, the Bears are not one of the final eight teams chasing Super Bowl dreams. But when it comes to fresh comfort food that is strong and consistent every year, Susie's is always at the top of its game. Bears management take notice.

Parisi's Drive In
6216 W 63rd Street, Chicago
773-586-5611   Rating:

I love this little white dog shack. It definitely has that yesteryear vibe to it. But hey, let's talk about the dog ($2.75). This is a Yummy Thummy for certain. You'll find the usual M7 suspects but with a huge cucumber wedge in place of the pickle. No argument there. If it were up to me, I'd consume cukes for breakfast, lunch, and dinner. For something different, order the Italian steak sandwich, one of the biggest sellers on the menu. This isn't your typical breaded steak sandwich. Rather, it's a hunk of steak topped with mozzarella and red sauce. A solid win at $5.30 or Wednesdays for $3.50.

Quick Bite Carry Outs
5155 N Western, Chicago
773-989-4918   Rating:

For thirty years now, Quick Bite had stood guard on the busy corner of Foster and Western. The owners, Tom and Pete Athanasakos, take care of the locals with flair. Grab a seat at the counter here and as you munch on your dog, you'll hear one of the owners barking out orders from memory for any of the regulars who traipse through the door. These guys know their people.

The dog itself is a tasty Pinky with the M7s all fresh and intact. For $5.99, the two dog special (with fries and a drink) is a steal. If you ate six dogs the day before and feel the need to vary your diet, try the Grilled Greek Chicken ($5.95) on French bread. It's definitely a keeper. A Vienna Beef Hall of Famer as of 2012. Cash only.

Around the corner

Two blocks south on Western (4955 N Western, Chicago) you'll find **Ash's Magic Shop**. This store has been around since the mid-80s and is one of only a handful of magic shops remaining in Chicago.

A definite throwback, the walls in this place are lined with gadgets, trick stuff, magic books, magic cards, gag gifts, and plenty of whooooppee cushions and fart perfumes. Ah yes, to be 10 years old again. There is also plenty of merchandise for the more seasoned magician.

Mr. Ash and his wife, Bonnie

Owners Ashod Baboorian (aka Mr. Ash) and his wife, Bonnie, run the shop and, hey, Mr. Ash has been on Bozo Circus nine times. Other than Bozo himself, Cookie and Mr. Ned, Mr. Ash likely tops the Bozo list for most visits. And the guy is downright funny. And I mean VERY funny. And Bonnie's got plenty of kick, too. When I asked her who the real boss was, she said, "Well, he's the one with all the magic experience. But I'm the only one around here with any brains. So it's definitely me." Ouch, Mr. Ash. Ouch.

Stop in and say, hello. You won't be sorry. Warning: As I mentioned, be prepared to laugh. Ask Mr. Ash a few questions and before you know it, he'll be coming at you with non-stop one-liners and stories. And check out the award-winning documentary on this place, *The Amazing Mr. Ash* at https://vimeo.com/86908002.

The Skyway Doghouse
9480 S Ewing, Chicago
773-731-2000

Rating:

This East Side gem is set on the corner of 95th and Ewing. For those of you who know little about Chicago's East Side, Ewing is 3600 East—as in 4.5 miles east of State Street. The Chicago dog (a Thummy at $3.19 with all the M7s and cucumber) comes with an excellent heaping of fries and has plenty of snap. Parking in this tiny lot can get jammed a bit during the lunch rush, but who cares? Your dog will be well worth it. A Vienna Beef Hall of Famer since 2006.

Around the corner

If you're in the mood for shrimp (and why wouldn't ya be?), **Calumet Fisheries** is just five blocks west on 95th street. Feeling the Surf and Turf? Snag a Skway dog and then order a half pound of shrimp ($9.45) from Calumet. Your taste buds will applaud. The fishery sits just above the Calumet River while the Skyway looms large to the west. Grab a seat along the sidewalk (or in your car), chow down, and take in the East Side sights.

After eating, I recommend a ride past the unassuming townhouse at **2319 E 100th Street**. As a former assistant state's attorney, I've read a good deal about **Richard Speck**, who, unfortunately, made this townhouse a sad part of our city's history. In 1966, Speck broke into this property and proceeded to kill eight of the nine nurses in the townhouse. The ninth escaped by hiding under a bed and later aimed her finger at Speck in open court and identified him as the killer. Speck received the death penalty but that sentence was later reversed on appeal. I am happy to report that Speck is no longer amongst the living. He died in 1998 at Statesville prison, just one day shy of his 50th birthday.

The Launching Pad
810 E Baltimore, Wilmington
815-476-6535   Rating:

This Route 66 eatery has a number of strong items on the menu. The Chicago Dog (a Thummy at $3.99) is a solid top seller, and though I feel rather treasonous saying this, the Carolina Slaw dog ($3.99 and topped with Carolina slaw, chili sauce, and Plochman's mustard) is just as good. There, I said it. Now don't shoot me. I suggest you do what I did–get one of each. It comes with your choice of either potato salad, apple sauce or chips.

The Pot roast sandwich ($8.99) is a winner and the Brunswick stew ($3.66 for a small, $5.66 for large) is mighty tasty. I took some stew home and my 20-year-old son knocked it off later that night and raved about it the following day.

Be sure to check out the wonderful historical pieces on the walls and don't go home without a picture of you standing beneath the Gemini Giant (the 28 foot tall fiberglass mascot). During the warmer months, the restaurant is open until 8. In the colder months—to 4. And in addition to being a restaurant, this place has a gift shop and a tiny Route 66 museum. Pieces of the past can be found all over this place and appeal to young and old alike.

The Lowdown

The Launching Pad - Home of the Giant

His time was nearing its end. He stood beside a run-down eatery that, to put it delicately, had fallen on hard times. So he stood there staring out at the cars passing along America's famed Route 66. The eatery was desolate and dark, abandoned for more than five years and looked like it was ready to be turned into a parking lot. And what of the man, the tall fiberglass man who stood beside the restaurant. Would he become a mound of rubble as well?

Well known to both the locals and to the thousands who flock to see him every year, the 28-foot tall Gemini Giant stands sentry on the edge of the Launching Pad, a Wilmington eatery roughly 15 miles and a few biscuit flips south of Joliet. Erected in 1965, he enjoyed a good life welcoming the comers and goers to town and into the restaurant for 47 years before the original owners, the Korlic family, sold the business. The subsequent owner let the business and building fall into disrepair and eventually left it empty for a period of five years.

The Gemini Giant

Enter Tully Garrett and his fiancé, Holly Barker. "It was a Thursday and we decided to go antiquing," Tully says. "Someone we knew suggested Wilmington so Wilmington it was. We had never been there before and as we approached the town, the first thing we saw was this huge fiberglass man. People were standing by him and taking pictures. So we pulled over."

"I walked over to the restaurant itself and peeked in, says Holly. "The place was spooky when we first saw it.

It was dark and musty, and looked liked it belonged on the set of a Jurassic Park movie."

Tully and Holy spoke to the folks they saw snapping photos of the Gemini Giant. "The people were from Egypt and another couple was from Amsterdam," Tully says. As Tully and Holly conversed with these people, another few cars rolled in. "These other people were from other countries and states too. Just out cruising Route 66. It was crazy."

After visiting the antique shops of Wilmington, Tully and Holly made their way out of town. Again they stopped when they saw more folks staring up at the Giant.

"This time I saw a for sale sign," says Holly. "I hadn't noticed that at first."

And yes, Tully and Holly eventually bought the business in 2017, much to the delight of the Gemini Giant who got a new paint job, courtesy of Tully and Holly. And if that were the end of the story, then that would be enough in and of itself. But there is more.

Tully, a native of the Lockport and Joliet areas met Holly, a North Carolinian, through an online grieving sight. Holly's husband, Jordon, lost an 8-year battle with cancer in 2014. He was 41. And Tully's wife, Nancy, died about the same time, another victim of cancer. She was 46.

"Grief is such a powerful force," says Holly. "When my husband died, I was completely lost. I felt compelled to write. And I reached out to others who were experiencing the same pain I was, and this led me to form, Grief Anonymous." An online organization dedicated to assisting those grieving the loss of a loved one, Grief

Anonymous has grown over the year and now has over 110,000 members and followers.

"Tully was grieving like me and then we found each other," Holly says. "I had been living in Canada with my husband but moved down south again after he died, to be with family. And Tully was here in the Midwest. We met and then things went great from there. After a while we knew we were right for each other and we knew we could help each other become whole again."

"Grief is such a difficult thing," adds Tully. "You're up, you're down. And there were five of us grieving."

Holly Barker and Tully Garret

And then came that ride to Wilmington. "After we saw the Gemini Giant we couldn't get him out of our heads," says Tully. "We talked it over and we decided to move on it." The couple pushed their careers to the side (insurance for Tully; pharmaceutical sales for Holly) and set their focus on the Launching Pad. "So we bought the place," Tully says. "Holly always wanted to run a café or restaurant and I loved the idea. And this place gives

Holly a base where she can continue her work with Grief Anonymous."

So Tully and Holly and their three children made daily trips from their home in New Lenox to Wilmington to get to work on restoring the Launching Pad to its 1960s diner glory. "We had contractors help with some of the work at first, but after that it was us, the five of us, putting in the time and labor," Tully says. "We spent some long days getting the place ready. But it was fun, and we were together."

After a year and a half of restoration work, Tully and Holly opened the restaurant in February of 2019. "The local community has been supportive and we had a large number of visitors from other states and all around the world who came here," says Tully. "Ninety-one countries were represented here in visits thus far this year."

"The Launching Pad has helped us meld as a family," Tully says as he becomes reflective. "We've all experienced so much pain and grief with the loss of our spouses and for our kids–the loss of their father or mother. Buying this place and working here has helped bring us together as a family. We have to continue to grow but being here, being a part of the re-birth of the Launching Pad has helped a great deal."

The Gemini Giant certainly seems to like his new owners. "We also like the idea of being part of something that is far greater than us," says Tully. "Route 66 is one of the great roads in America. It starts in Chicago and goes to LA. It is 100% Americana and it will be here for years to come–long after we're gone. But while we're here, we're preserving a piece of America's thumbprint and we're very proud to be a part of that."

When Holly and Tully first saw the Gemini Giant on

their antiquing day trip in September of 2017, little did they know that he would help heal their wounds. Strange what brings people together. Holly and Tully lost each other's soul mates and then found each other. They went out looking for antiques and instead found a tall, fiberglass man—a man, perhaps, with special powers, a man who brings people together and watches them, through sweat and effort and love, grow and become a new family.

Mr. D's Shish Kabob

6656 W Diversey, Chicago

773-637-0042   Rating:

I never thought I'd be putting a place with "Shish Kabob" in its name in a hot dog book, but Mr. D's is more than worthy. Justin Heath, the director of policy for Alderman Gilbert Villegas (34th Ward), shot me a note directing me to this joint. And I must say, Justin knows his stuff when it comes to dog discoveries. He also turned me on to the Chubby Wieners (page 98). During my travels as a Streets and San guy, I hit countless hot dog joints, but I missed Mr. D's. Thanks to my new friend at the 34th Ward, I'll be returning again, again, and again in the future.

When I walked through the door of this tiny, homey restaurant, mom and son were working the grill. Dad had an apron wrapped across his chest but was taking a break at a table talking to customers. Wonderful smells filled the air as a steak sandwich and a sausage split down the middle sizzled on the grill. Wowza. From the workers, to the look, to the aura, Mr.D's is the epitome of a mom and pop diner. As for the dog ($3.40 with all of the M7s sans the pickle), it was scrumdillyicious and came with a large heaping of the best fresh cut fries I have encountered.

Red Hot Ranch
2072 N Western, Chicago
773-772-6030   Rating:

For a dog with a tremendous snap, Red Hot Ranch is the place to go. This Pinky ($3.62 with tasty fresh cut fries) is mighty good and comes lightly charred. Everything includes mustard, onions, relish, and sport peppers. One of the main things I like about the Ranch is that light char. It's not a 10 minute fiasco as is the case at most char dog shacks. This baby retains the snap and adds a bit of burn to the skin to create an interesting taste.

Jacky's
5415 S Pulaski, Chicago
773-767-7676   Rating:

A core eatery in the West Elsdon neighborhood since the late-70s, Jacky's has a mighty tasty dog. For $3.49, you get a Pinky with all the M7 trimmings and fries. The dog is the definite winner on the menu, but if you're in the mood for something else, try the Big Baby ($3.49). This is not like other dime-a-dozen Big Baby's. Featured on *Chicago's Best*, this double cheeseburger comes out with a mound of grilled onions guaranteed to put a smile on your face. If you have time, grab a stool at the grill and have a chat with Pat. She'll make sure you have some fun.

The Lowdown
Jacky's – Keep on Dreaming

Take a good look at that photo on the next page of Patricia Koutsoubas, the co-owner of Jacky's at 54th and Pulaski. See that welcoming smile, the twinkle in her eye. If you pull in even closer and give her another look, you'll see something else—something altogether different: the face of the American dream.

In 1969, at age 18, Pat left Greece and came directly to Chicago where she lived with her cousins in the Marquette Park area. "I was just a kid getting used to a new place, a new country. But I was thankful for my cousins. They let me stay with them for five years."

During that time, Pat went to school and worked. "My cousin ran a little hot dog and burger place on 58th and Kedzie. My parents were hard working people who taught me to work hard and to always be kind and truthful." Pat applied that same work ethic and attitude as she went to work for her cousin. That dog and burger joint eventually became the beloved Nicky's – the Real McCoy (not the imposter), owned by Pat's brother and located just across the street from its original home. "I learned the business working for family in that place."

Pat's husband, John Koutsoubas, emigrated three years before Pat. They met on the South Side and not long after that, they got married and then opened Jacky's in 1977.

Pat Koutsoubas

"It was difficult at first. There was a large Polish community here in those days, and other groups too. We were a new business and people didn't know us. But we put in long days and made quality food. The local people saw this and I think they respected that. They started to come in and things got better." The hot dog and the Big Baby were the two top sellers in those days and remain big sellers today.

Jacky's was featured on *Chicago's Best* for its classic Big Baby double cheeseburger in 2015. "Lots of places offer the Big Baby, but it's not the same as the burger we make here. Ours is best. I do not skimp on quality. If it means it costs us more, so be it. Money is second. The customer is first and the customer deserves top quality."

When first starting out, John and Pat, typically worked 18 hour days. "It was just the two of us back then. And we were just planning to work to ten at night but guys who worked the third shift at the truck docks down the street asked us to stay open later. So we did that back then (open until 1:45 AM). And we still stay open late now."

After Pat gave birth to her two children, she stayed home for five years to raise them. "My husband was handling everything back then. Every day, he was putting in 18 hours. I felt bad that I wasn't able to help him, but I was raising the kids."

When her daughter was three, Pat returned to Jacky's full time. "I was glad to ease the burden on my husband. My mother and other family members helped with the kids.

Pat and John's children are now grown. "My son Constantino is a corporate lawyer and my daughter Maggie is a banker. The kids are both hard-workers. I always told them that you have to work for what you want. I told them not to expect any handouts from anyone. And they saw my husband always working here. Always working to take care of his family. I think they learned from that. But I regret that I missed family time with my kids when they were young. We were both always working. But my kids know that we didn't put in those hours to buy lots of material things for ourselves. We did it for them. But still, I have that regret of not being with them more when they were young."

After years of hard work and long hours, John

suffered a severe back injury. "He went through three surgeries. It's been tough on him. He now has difficulty using one leg and he can't stand for long on it." As a result, John has not been able to work at Jacky's for over ten years.

But that injury also came with a blessing. "John missed out on being with our kids when they were young, because he was always working. Always. But now, we have grandchildren. And my husband gets to see them often. And he's spoiling them. We both are." Pat smiles. "I'm only working 2 to 3 days a week now. I want to be with my grandkids as much as possible, too. They bring me great joy."

That being said, Pat has no plans to retire. She's still working on the balancing act between family and work. "I like to work and I like my restaurant. I like meeting different people. I get to talk and have fun with my customers and the people who work here with me. And sometimes I give advice but only if I am asked to give it."

Pat moves to the grill to adjust a flame. It's almost 10 AM−opening time. "I could never be a couch person and just stare at the TV all day. I need to be around people. I need to keep moving. And then when I am with my grandchildren, I can sit back and relax and enjoy them."

Yes, Pat's is the face of the American Dream. As you look at her face, perhaps you can see a bit of your own, or the face of your parents or grandparents−folks who came to this country to make a better life than they had in their homeland. Pat arrived, she worked hard, she raised a wonderful family and now she and John get to spoil their grandkids.

Superdawg Drive In

6682 N Northwest Highway, Chicago

773-763-0660   Rating:

Superdawg's place in Chicago hot dog history cannot be disputed. For over 70 years, this dog joint has churned out mountains of Superdawgs ($6.40 with fries) from the same tri-corner on the far Northwest Side. And what about the legendary Superdawg itself? Well, this is no ordinary dawg. Not by any means. This ¼ pounder has tremendous snap and flavor, and comes on an oversized poppy seed bun. Mustard, relish, onions, and zesty peppers top the dog. Can you say YUMMY?

Though original owners Maurie and Flaurie Berman are no longer around to run the show, their family still carries the dog tradition forward. And Maurie and Flaurie, in their hot dog personas, can still be found atop the roof welcoming all visitors to this local institution.

Dave's Red Hots

4000 W Roosevelt, Chicago

773-722-9935   Rating:

This unpretentious stand offers a dog with plenty of bark and snap with fries for $3.90. If you go with everything, your pinky will be covered with all of the M7s except for tomatoes and celery salt. One of

Chicago's oldest stands, this Vienna Beef Hall of Famer has been churning out dogs for over 80 years and is a West Side mainstay.

Wiener Circle
2622 N Clark, Chicago
773-477-7444   Rating:

A Lincoln Park fixture, this joint is as well known for its frisky late night work staff as they are for their dogs (a tasty Pinky at $4.50). Be sure to read the sign out in front of the stand. The wordsmith always has some creative words to share. If you're with the family or if you're trying to impress your future in-laws with your knowledge of the Chicago dog, go during the daylight hours. This joint stays open to 4-5A.M. and caters to drunk eaters later in the day, especially as the nearby bars close. If you're up for such hilarity, go there and partake in some abuse. This Vienna Beef Hall of Famer also has 35th Street Red Hots and Red Hot Ranch in their stable.

Consigliere No. 1
Hot Tip from Tony the Hat

A city electrician for 30-plus years, Tony the Hat doesn't know what a brown bag looks like. "I eat at places all over the city. Every damn day. I know all the good spots." I'm a firm believer in giving credit where credit is due: no truer words from a guy named The Hat have ever been spoken. When I undertook the research (lunch eating) that led to my first book, *The Streets and San Man's Guide to Chicago Eats*, The Hat was one of my main lunch partners. Back then, he turned me on to a bunch of different eateries, including the Wiener Circle. He's a big fan.

"Get the Polish and tell 'em to char it," the Hat says. "Tell 'em to put the usual mustard and grilled onions on it. But then, have 'em top it off with some hot giardiniera." Tony smiles. "That's the key. That's a damn good sandwich and it'll set your ass on fire."

Hat's Wiener Circle visits are generally in the day, but he strays every now and again. "I been there for the show at night, too. It's some funny shit. Most of the time, the workers are the only ones throwing the insults around. The best, though, is when you get some guy just drunk enough to still be on his A-game and then he gets into it with the workers. That's the best. You just chew on your hot dog or Polish and sit back and laugh." There you have it: The Hat has spoken.

The Duck Inn
2701 S Eleanor, Chicago
312-724-8811   Rating:

Where to begin? Oh let me count the ways. First off, to call this creation a hot dog is an injustice of huge proportions. The Duck Inn Dog ($10 or $5 during Oh-So

Happy Hour, 5-6pm) goes far above and beyond the basic hot dog in size and flavor, and has an incredible snap at first bite. Made with a blend of all-natural beef and duck fat, this oversized dog will have you doing cartwheels up and down the sidewalks on your street for days.

Most big dogs/sausages are rather heavy, but this dog has a much lighter feel to it, and it's melt-in-your-mouth good. And hey, what about the jewels that go atop this bad boy? Chef Kevin Hickey adds homemade pickles, relish and mustard along with his creative use of onions and tomatoes. And keep a glass of water at the ready if you dare to munch on the oh-so hot peppers (Yummy). Though this joint is known for its rotisserie duck ($65), this is a hot dog book and I can't have you spending your kid's college funds on duck. But then again, if the kids are grown or if that child of yours decides to go to trade school, then, hey, it's time to get after that duck. If you're going to do the Duck Inn Dog, be sure to try the tasty and pillowy-soft duck fat fries. Put the duck wings ($12, $6 during Happy Hour) on your list, too. They're tasty as hell in the Japanese BBQ sauce. **Happy Hour is 5-6PM Tuesday-Friday**, where all bevies and items from the Classic menu (including the dog) are half price. Yowzah. **Other location:** at Time Out Market.

The Lowdown
The Duck Inn – A Family Tradition

So how does a Michelin award-winning, former executive chef at the Ritz Carlton come to create his version of the beloved Chicago style hot dog? And why exactly would he park his newest venture, The Duck Inn, in Bridgeport rather than at some Fancy Dan North Side location?

Most hot dog fanatics out there may know little about Kevin Hickey, but within the confines of the Chicago food scene, Kevin is a major star. A Chicago native, Kevin showcased his top-notch culinary wares through the years in such places as Beverly Hills, London, Dublin, and more while working for Four Seasons. He returned to Chicago when offered the opportunity to become the Executive Chef at the Ritz Carlton.

The Duck Inn

"I had a strong desire to return to Chicago and make my mark as a chef," Kevin says. "I also wanted my son to grow up surrounded by family."

In 2014, Kevin opened The Duck Inn on the near South Side, in the very same Bridgeport neighborhood where he was raised. In fact, Kevin now lives on the very same block he grew up on. That, my friends, is some definite small world stuff. And the name of his restaurant—it bears the same name as the bus stop diner his great grandmother ran at 35th and Ashland during the depression.

"It's still very surreal for me. I never thought I would do what I've done. But it means a lot to me as my family has been business owners in Bridgeport since the 19th century, so I feel a strong need to not let it die with me."

The Duck Inn was voted one of the three Top Chicago restaurants to open by *Esquire* in 2015. Since then it has continued to rack up awards by the boatloads for its duck, hip atmosphere, ultra-cool beer garden, great beer and cocktail selections, and, ah yes—The Duck Inn Dog.

"I first created it (the dog) for a Crosstown Classic themed charity event at the Four Seasons and it was a huge hit. But my old school European Hotelier boss wouldn't let me put it on the menu. He felt it was not appropriate at a luxury setting."

I would expect nothing less from a high brow European hotel boss. The guy probably still thinks the world is flat, too.

"Once he (the boss) left, I put it on the menu and it was quite the sensation. When I decided to leave to open The Duck Inn, the dog had become a part of my personal brand so I wanted to bring it with."

Before I write another word, I feel compelled to say this: Hot Dog fans, do not go another week without making an excursion to Bridgeport for this mouth-watering delight. It's that damn good. If you prefer, you can put your kicks on and head over to the Time Out Market (916 West Fulton) instead where you can try several different variations of The Duck Inn dog.

"Time Out Market is a really dynamic environment and a perfect setting for Duck Inn Dogs. Hot dogs and French fries made with a commitment to quality and creativity with a strong respect for tradition."

Tradition. There it is again. The word Kevin knows a lot about. "My father all but pounded into me the need for honesty and integrity in the work you do. He taught me that the only thing I really had in the world was my name and my word, and to make God damn sure it means something."

Hickey. The Duck Inn. Duck Inn Dogs. Three names that certainly "mean something" to the wonderful world of Chicago foodies. How lucky we are.

Snappy Dog
6682 N Northwest Highway, Chicago
773-775-7600   Rating:

This dog shack may be the size of a shoebox but it kicks out a scrumdillicious dog (a $4 Pinky includes fresh cut fries) with all of the M7s. Give the Snappy Dog (1/4 all beef monster with secret hot sauce and cheese, $5.75 with fries) a try, if you're in the need for a bigger dog. But if you find yourself in a St. Patty's Day mood, try the Irish Beef sandwich ($6.50 with fries). This hot corned beef on a pretzel roll with mustard, horseradish or thousand island sauce is mighty tasty and may just cause you to start dancing an Irish jig for joy.

Windy City Hot Dogs
4205 W 63rd Street, Chicago
773-581-0332   Rating:

MMM

This dog stand has been taking care of the West Lawn locals for almost 20 years now. The solid dog (a Pinky for $2.90) comes with fresh M7s and has plenty of snap on a plain, steamed bun. Feeling the need for a bigger dog? As they say here at Windy City, GO LONG. Their foot long dog comes with a salad of goodies atop it and fries for $6.25. Yummy with a Capital Y.

Around the corner

Just two blocks away, my guy, **Big Chief**–as he is known to the West Lawn locals, is the cigar store Indian who holds court atop the roof on the northwest corner of 63rd and Pulaski. Gone is the cigar store, replaced at first by an optometrist center (hence, the spectacles) and now a dental center. This guy is one of my all-time favorite West Lawners and he also offers one of my favorite optical illusions.

In the days of old, after a night of bevvies on 63rd Street, I'd climb atop the roof to get to know Chief a bit better. He's a good guy, but rather quiet. It always seemed like I was the one doing the talking. And he never thanked me when I'd yank out some of the arrows that ne'er-do-wells had fired into his back. Even then, just as quiet as can be. But the big fella is also a magician. Stand just off the southwest corner, directly across from Marco's barbershop (4008 W 63rd Street) and give Big Chief a gander. What he'll show you is guaranteed to bring on the giggles. At first glance, it looks like Chief has his dillywagger hanging out of his zipper. But as you inch a bit further east, you'll see that what you thought looked like his unit is actually his left thumb. Big Chief has been around for well over 50 years and is always worthy of a gander.

Big Chief

Gone but not forgotten. At 4016 W 63rd, there once stood, **The Midget Club**, a bar run by Parnell St. Aubin, a Munchkin soldier from the Disney classic, *The Wizard of Oz.* With his wife, Mary Ellen, they ran this bar at this location (it had been at 6356 S Kedzie before that) for almost 30 years. I had the pleasure of having a beer in the club twice, and enjoyed the Oz history present in the assorted photographs on the walls. The club was shut down in 1982 to make room for the West Lawn Library. I guess you have to call that progress.

Joey's Red Hots
11500 S Western, Chicago
773-614-8997   Rating:

Usually things start off in the city and then migrate to the burbs, or start in the burbs and stay there. Not so with Joey's. They opened two places in Orland Park and then later, in 2018, they made their entry into the South Side. Since then, the place has been moving butts in and out faster than you can say, NEXT.

Joey's offers a solid Pinky dog with all of the M7s fresh and in place. The dog comes with fries for a bargain price of $2.65. One of my other favorites here is the Philly cheese steak, a whopper of a sandwich for $5.75.

Around the corner

Just one block south you will find **Beverly Records** (11612 S Western). Run by the **Dreznes brothers** since 1967, this is the place to visit for that oldie or latest release on vinyl. And hey, they even carry local hit songs by small time bands. Pop in and have some fun flipping through the stacks.

Dog House Grill
1534 N Wells, Chicago
312-631-3737   Rating:

This Old Town haunt serves up a solid hot dog ($3.69), with one of the best presentations I received in the city (the dog maker arranged the tomatoes and sport peppers atop the other ingredients in a way that made it look like a living, breathing piece of art). I was almost reluctant to ruin this piece of art with my teeth. But I overcame that notion and thoroughly enjoyed the dog.

In the late '60s when I was a munchkin, my older sister used to take me to Old Town to go visit the poster and record shops. The smell of incense was everywhere. In the '90s, a gypsy fortune teller on Wells Street spilled some bad news on me, and I've been hiding from the Old Town ever since. But a buddy hit me up with this recommendation, and I must say, it was well worth the trip. And I think that gypsy curse has been broken.

Branko's Sandwich Shop
1118 W Fullerton, Chicago
773-472-4873   Rating:

Just a football toss away from DePaul University, this stand could be the virtual poster child for mom and pop restaurants. The Branko family has run this place since the mid-1970s. And as for the dog itself, it's a delicious Thummy ($3.26) with plenty of snap and comes with all of the M7s (with round pickles instead of a spear). This dog had a rather unique taste to it and is a definite winner.

The Ninos family originally ran a sub shop at this location. When the Brankos took over, they continued to make the subs the same way, using the same ingredients that the Ninos clan did before them. With fresh meats, cheeses, veggies, and D'Amato bread, the sub is scrumdillyicious ($6 range for the subs). Give it a shot.

The Lowdown
Branko's Sandwich Shop – Call me Mama

With this iconic sandwich shop in the shadows of DePaul University, as you would expect, many students have visited Branko's over the years for a sub, a dog, a burger, a chicken sandwich, or whatever else they might order from Branko's extensive menu. In addition to the food they receive, these students (and other patrons, as well) may also get a piece of Andja Branko's mind—and it's a fine mind, indeed. You would be hard-pressed to find a person as hard-working, honest, and dutiful as Andja.

"I treat everybody with respect," Andja says, "and I let them now that they are loved. And I expect people in the restaurant to be respectful too." For the students who visit regularly, many have become almost adopted children to Andja.

Andja Branko

"I bring them in and I read their papers. I make notes on how to improve them. I try to help them with their schooling to get better grades. To get jobs," Andja says. She also admits that she gravitates towards some students and others who may be experiencing difficulties. "I can see it in their face, if they have problems. It is not hard to see. I tell them that it will be okay. I tell them to work hard and I let them know that their lives mean something. That they are worthwhile. When someone is hurting, they need to know that. And I tell them to call me, 'Mama.'"

Along with her parents and three sisters, Andja, now 59, emigrated from Yugoslavia in the mid-1970s. She was 15 at the time. "I was so happy in Yugoslavia. We lived in the center of a town called, Srbobran. I took classes in Eastern European dance. I loved music and I loved to dance. And I loved spending time with my grandfather. He was a quiet man who understood me. When we came here to America, it took some time to get used to everything."

When the Brankos first arrived they lived on Chicago's East Side and along with her parents, Andja went to work for her aunt and uncle every day at the now defunct Continental Bakery at 105th and Ewing. "My aunt and uncle were very good to us. They helped us get started here."

In addition to going to high school, learning a new language, and working for her aunt and uncle, as the eldest of four children Andja also helped take care of her three younger sisters as they grew up. She applied that same motherly instinct when I arrived at Brankos. Andja invited me into the rest area behind the grill station, where she set a place for me at a small table and offered me a cup of tea. A welcoming person, a nice person, but make no mistake about it—Andja is also a no nonsense person. "If someone says something inappropriate or acts disrespectful in this restaurant, I bring them a bag for their food and return their money, and tell them to leave and not return again."

And sure, many students and others who have made Brankos a regular stopping spot over the years have called her, Mama, as per her request. But so do her own two children.

"I put in a lot of time working at this restaurant," Andja says, "but when I had my daughter and later my son, things started to make more sense to me. It was always work, work, work. But when I had my kids, I knew what I was meant to be. I was meant to be a mother. I think I developed that instinct young, when I was watching over my sisters."

Sure enough Andja helped care for her three sisters when they were young and made sure they did their homework each day by having them sit in a booth at Branko's and overseeing their work. She had her own children do the same thing.

Andja is proud of her children. The words she shares with her adopted DePaul students, she shares with her own children too. "They know they are loved. They know they are important and worthwhile. My daughter is a strong woman. A good woman. You can't push her around and she has done well. She is happily married and she's an accountant. She lives in Rolling Meadows. My son is truly my angel. He is a good person and I am so proud of him. My husband is also a hard-working man. He works for Northeastern Illinois University as a groundskeeper."

Andja's parents still live in the apartment above Branko's. In their 80s now, they both have severe medical issues requiring constant attention. "We have help in the day for them but I stay here 24/7 and work down here in the day and then help them at night."

When I asked Andja how many hours a week she works at Branko's and caring for her parents, her answer came quick. "Over 100 hours a week. But I do not say that to complain. It's just how it is. I work the family business and I take care of my parents. It is the right thing to do. Besides, I don't sleep much. My dad always said I was like a bird, a bird that could sleep on one leg on a tree limb."

In her spare time, Andja still loves participating in Eastern European dance with the Chicago ensemble, Balkanske Igre. Her son is also a nationally ranked dancer, and she has enjoyed going to various dance events over the years.

While her sisters take care of the major business decisions, Andja is the Branko who is always on site, seven days per week, the one who runs the show—solo. That's right, solo. She cooks, she takes orders, she cleans, she mops the floors, she chats with customers. In short, she has given, and continues to give, her heart and soul to this business that her family built. But behind it all, as she says, her favorite job is being a mother.

"I am not perfect. But I try hard to be a good person. A respectful person. And I love my children. I am working on writing a book. I call it, 'The Joy of Mother-hood.' We are all special people. We cannot focus on the negative. We must stress the positive."

To her own children and to her adopted DePaul children, they know Andja speaks the truth. And they know that they have one hell of a Mama.

Martin's Corner
2058 W 23rd Place, Chicago
773-847-5515   Rating:

Imagine this: A corner tavern that doles out good booze and quality craft beer adds a tiny grill directly next door. That's what Bob Martin did in 1985 and Martin's Corner has been kicking out enough quality dogs since then to become a member of the Vienna Beef Hall of Fame (2015). This Pinky ($3.35 with fries) is solid and holds all the M7 ingredients. This joint rocks the pizza on Friday and Saturday nights and they make a pie with solid taste. Sure you can step into the grill and grab your chow to go, but c'mon, be brave. Step through that bar door and get yourself a bevvie and order your chow. The bartender might sneer at you but then again, maybe she won't. Rumor has it that she last smiled in the year 2014. Just keep your big boy or big girl pants on and enjoy the food and beer.

Around the corner

I'm about to get churchy on you here, but hang in there. It won't last for long. Kitty corner to Martin's stands **St. Paul Catholic church.** This 1897 beauty is huge both inside and out. Give it a gander. Then pop into St. Pius V Catholic church (1901 S Ashland) home of the shrine of St. Jude, the patron saint of lost causes. Folks come from all over to visit and pray to St. Jude. I went there a few times over the years, including to get help to graduate from law school, and Jude delivered. Thanks again, Jude. You're the best. Okay, that's the end of my churchin'. But know this–your Sunday obligation and mine have now been met.

St. Paul Catholic church

One more thing: Just three blocks away at 24th and Oakley (the **Heart of Chicago** neighborhood), you'll find five top-notch Italian restaurants that will fill your belly with excellent food and treat your pocketbook right. **Ignotz** (the Linguine and clams, $14.50, is my Go To), **Bacchanalia**, **Brunas**, **La Fontanella**, and **Il Vicinato** (with melt in your mouth homemade veal ravioli in meat sauce, $14; and the best antipasto salad on the South

Side. Share it for $6 per person). If you haven't been to 24th and Oakley, you simply haven't lived.

Wrigleyville Dogs
3737 N Clark, Chicago
773-296-1500   Rating:

Ah yes, the beauty of knocking down a pre-game or post-game dog just a few feet from Wrigley Field. This dog shack kicks out a wide variety of food (subs, sandwiches, shisk kabob platters, and more), but my Go To here is still the hot dog. This Thummy ($4.05) has all of the M7s and has solid snap. Though this dog is solid, it may also be one of the most expensive classic dogs in the city (but hey, everything in Cubbyville is expensive, so deal with it). For almost 30 years now, Wrigleyville Dogs has been offering solid food. For something different, and for only $7.00, give the baked chicken leg meal a shot (comes with garlic bread, rice, fries and potatoes).

Donald's Famous Hot Dogs
2325 S Western, Chicago
773-254-7777   Rating:

There are two Donald's dog joints in Chicago and one

in Westchester, and they all offer a snappy Pinky ($3) with all of the M7 fixins. I've munched dogs at the Pilsen location (address above) and the Garfield Ridge location at 48th and Central. Both offer the same solid products. If your stomach is craving something other than a dog, no problem. I suggest any of the daily soup specials. All are solid and not many fast food joints have a different soup each day. Want more? The pork chop sandwich ($5.29) is always a winner.

Around the corner

If you need to visit your Aunt Martha or Uncle Ben at Cook County Jail, here's the good news: you're less than a mile away. Though the address is 2700 S California (and yes, that's where you'll enter to see your dear auntie or uncle), I suggest taking a ride along the backside of the jail – right down Sacramento from 26th Street. It's far less congested than California and you can cruise at a slow pace and take in the sights: barbed wire, watch towers, walls and buildings. This place is enormous and yet it's still overcrowded. A drive down Sacramento is an eye opener any day of the year. Perhaps, you'll see some hoopers in the yard on a warm day; perhaps you'll hear the bark of a guard or an inmate; perhaps you'll hear utter silence; or perhaps you'll see your Uncle Ben tunneling his way under one of the walls. Heed this advice: ease on down the road and leave Uncle Ben behind.

Fat Johnnies
7242 S Western, Chicago
773-633-8196

Rating:

"Oh Fat Johnnies, how I love thee. Let me count thy ways."
–Billy Shakespeare

This is the consummate Chicago hot dog shack. John originally served dogs from a cart just a few blocks away, and his stand is built upon that same cart concept– a steam table but no fryers. In other words, if you're a Fat Johnnies newbie, don't come looking for French fries cuz you won't find any here. What you'll find instead, as the regulars know, is one of the TOP hot dogs in the city.

This is a David Berg Thummy ($2.50) with some of the best damn M7s (cucumber instead of a pickle) you will ever taste. Fresh. Fresh. Fresh. And always tasty. If you want to up the ante, try the Mighty Dog ($), a tamale split open on a bun with a hot dog dropped inside of it, and then smothered with chili and cheese and the M7s. This is a meal that can carry you through an 8-hour day. Trust me.

The Lowdown
Fat Johnnies – Flowers or Hot Dogs

John 'Fat Johnnie' Pawlikowki has been slinging some of the best dogs in Chicago for over 50 years now. If you stepped up to his stand at 72nd and Western, you'd likely fall in line behind some Streets and San workers, Com Ed guys, salesmen from the new and used car dealers on Western, or some locals from the neighborhood. And when it came your turn to order, you could peer though the order window and see the man of girth who runs the show, clad in his apron. Fat Johnnie is to the Hot Dog world what Michael Jordan is to basketball.

After bouncing out of Harper High school a wee bit early, John went to work at the Nabisco plant at 73rd and Kedzie, just up the street from Marquette Park. Not long after starting the job, the truck drivers at Nabisco went on strike. Unsure of what to do, John figured his days at Cookie Central were numbered. That's when an old-timer at Nabisco told John he had a hot dog cart he'd sell him for a few hundred bucks.

Fat Johnnies

"I jumped at the chance," John said."That was in 1968 and I was a young buck. I started my hot dog business with that cart at the corner of 69th and Damen. But I didn't have a name for my business back then."

John's parents, John and Stella, ran a gardening business on a lot at 72nd and Western, directly beside where Fat Johnnie's now stands. "They were there for over 40 years running the business," says John. "I never gave much thought to taking over. My brother Frank and me, we just couldn't see ourselves doing the same thing that they did."

In 1972 John approached his father with the idea of opening up a full-blown Hot Dog stand on Western. "My dad wasn't quite sure about the idea. But he said he would give me the land to use but only if my brother went in on it with me."

So Frank and Johnnie had a pow wow. "But Frank didn't need much convincing. He was sold on the idea." With everything set in stone, all the brothers needed was a name for their stand. Frank and John grabbed seats at a table with a bottle of VO whiskey to work their way through the potential names. The final choices: 'Frank and Johnnies' or 'Fat Johnnies.' "Neither one of us really cared much for Frank and Johnnies when it came down to it, so we just went with Fat Johnnies. And once that was decided, we shook hands and then we finished off the bottle of VO."

The stand officially opened on May 12, 1972. Over the years, the hot dog and the chili cheese dog have been the biggest sellers. "Other people can say what they want, but I invented the chili cheese dog. Right here at Fat Johnnies." So be it. Hot Dog royalty has spoken.

Johnnies' son Teddy, a hot dog guru in his own right and a mainstay at Fat Johnnies over the years, passed away in April of 2019, a loss that weighs heavily on John. And John is still battling his way through a couple of medical issues. "Both of my knees are shot. I guess it's finally time to get the replacements." But John has no immediate intention of retiring. "I love this place and I love seeing my customers." And those customers come from near and far. "We've had people here from Japan, Ireland, Korea, Germany–from a bunch of countries. And then we get our regulars and first-timers too."

Johnnie will turn 72 in 2020. He says that he has eaten at least one hot dog every day since he opened his cart in 1968. "And my ticker's in good shape and my cholesterol level is still perfect." And then Johnnie adds, "And never once did I put ketchup on my own hot dog."

Hot G Dog
5009 N Clark, Chicago
773-209-336   Rating:

MMM1/2

When encased meats guru Doug Sohn shut down Hot Doug's in late 2014, the closing sent a shock wave through Chicago's encased meats world. Gone were the assorted Sohn dog/sausage creations and the supremely tasty duck fat fries. *Voila.* Former Hot Doug's cooks, brothers Juan Carlos Garcia and Octavio Garcia (Hot "G" for Garcia), opened this place in 2015 and they have resurrected a number of dogs/sausages that Hot Doug's lovers raved about. Try the Thuringer ($4.55 for this pork and beef based garlic dog). And keep on the lookout for the specialty dogs like the Duck sausage dog ($9) and Alligator dog ($9). If you go on a weekend you can get some duck fat fries too. Yummy. This place isn't Hot Doug's but it is awfully darn good.

Consigliere No. 2
Hot Tip from Kayleigh the Crab

 Having grown up in Maryland, where everyone either eats crab legs or crab cakes on a daily basis, or has a pet crab that they take for slow, afternoon walks, Kayleigh the Crab took a liking to the Chicago dog after arriving on the North Side almost three years ago, at age 25. As a Chicago transplant, she was well aware of the Chicago dog's local status.

"The Chicago dog, boosted in part by its reputation and the love this city has for it, is definitely better than any dog I've tried out East."

A Lakeview Millennial who shares her creative juices for a River North advertising firm, Kayleigh the Crab has knocked down her fair share of hot dogs over the last few years.

"I had my first hot dog at Murphy's Red Hots (a legendary but now closed stand) just off the corner of Belmont and Racine within a month of moving here."

Though she's a fan of the traditional Chicago dog, Kayleigh the Crab also has taken a liking to something a wee bit different–the Andouille sausage at Hot G.

"I love the portion, flavor and caramelized onions on top. The sausage itself has some cayenne, garlic, and maybe some fennel. And paprika too. Very tasty."

And how about the wide variety of Hot G mustards, Kayleigh?

"They offer many different mustards. I had brown mustard on mine. But if brown mustard and caramelized onions don't appeal to you, you can pick from a long list of other hot dog toppings, and traditional Chicago hot dog toppings."

There you have it. Kayleigh the Crab has spoken. So get out to Hot G and try that Andouille sausage. And be sure to get it with brown mustard and caramelized onions. You won't go wrong. And who knows? You just might find Kayleigh the Crab there. Rumor has it that she goes to Hot G often where she stands in line waiting with baited breath for the arrival of the Maryland Crab dog. No doubt we'll see that on the Hot G menu soon.

Lu Lu's Hot Dogs
1000 S Leavitt, Chicago
312-243-3444   Rating:

Not only will you get a great dog (a $3 Pinky with fries) from Lu Lu's, but you may also get a free comedy show. When I asked who the head honcho was, one of the guys working the counter (who just so happened to be one of the head honchos but wasn't about to disclose it) said, "SHE's upstairs shaving. And it might take a while. She usually cuts herself up pretty good." The others working the counter had a good laugh at that one, as did I. Yeah, that's the way I like it: a solid dog and some free comedy from the guys slapping the mustard on the dog. It doesn't get any better than that. Unless of course you want to try the Italian beef. One of my favorites in Chicago ($5.50). This joint has been around since 1968 and is a 2017 Vienna Beef Hall of Famer.

Around the corner

There are all kinds of county, state and federal office buildings within a few blocks of Lu Lu's. Isn't that exciting? The **VA's Regional office** is at 2122 W Taylor (go there if your Uncle Ed needs some help getting his Viet Nam papers in order; I'm sure the wait will be short), **Juvy Court** is at 1100 S Hamilton (they have wanted posters of a young Tony The Hat plastered all over the walls), and the **FBI Field office** is at 2111 W Roosevelt (with more photos of Tony the Hat on their walls).

George's Gyros
3445 South Halsted, Chicago
773-247-4770   Rating:

MMM1/2

As long as I'm touting Tony the Hat's accomplishments, I have to add that he turned me on to this Bridgeport stronghold. For $2.50 you'll get a solid Pinky with plenty of flavor and all the M7s. I got mine charred, as per Tony's suggestion, and it was damn good. This is a mom (Elaine) and daughter (Athena) show here and they take care of the city workers, cops, and locals who flock to this joint. Grab a seat at the counter, snag a small soup (a bargain at $2), and munch on that char dog. Yummy.

INTERMISSION

After knocking off a bunch of dogs, I usually need a break. Maybe I'll do some reading or I might take my hounds for a walk or I might bark at some neighborhood kids while I coach them in lacrosse. And so, as a reward for making it halfway through this book, it's time for you to take a well-deserved break. And for your pleasure I have two intermission toys for you on the following six pages.

Welcome To

The Battle

OF THE FIBERGLASS HOT DOG MASCOTS

Final Four – MMA Style

Bout No. 1 Contestants: From the far reaches of Will County, the **Gemini Giant** from The Launching Pad vs. Northsiders **Maurie and Flaurie** from Superdawg.

Sorry Superdawg. This is no contest. The Gemini Giant is 28-feet tall and is a solid, barrel-chested stud. Not only that but he holds a sizeable rocket in his bulging arms. And what do you have? A couple of 12-foot wiener waifs. Sure Maurie is trying hard to look rough and tumble in his Tarzan suit but, c'mon, when you compare his arms to the Gemini Giant's they look like spaghetti noodles. And Flaurie won't help much. Sure she'll spin around a few times in an attempt to distract the Giant a bit with her pleated skirt and sexy bow atop her noggin, but that simply won't do it. The Gemini Giant is all about focus. After a couple of rocket slams to their noggins, the Gemini Giant brings home the easy victory:

Winner: **The Gemini Giant** by Knock Out - 25 seconds into the first round.

Bout 2. Contestants: Northsider supreme **Wolfy's Hot Dog on a Fork** vs **Big Chief** from 63rd and Pulaski.

Before we start, I get it. You're probably saying, Hey, Big Chief, as he is affectionately known by his cohorts in the West Lawn neighborhood, isn't even a hot dog mascot. I agree. Sure he was originally a cigar store mascot, and then an optometry store mascot before taking on his current role atop a dental center. But to all that, I say, who gives a flyin' crap? This is Chicago, for Jiminy Cricket's sake, and Big Chief has some local political friends in high places. So sit down, be quiet and just accept it. Big Chief is in the bout.

At first glance, you can't help but notice how tall the Wolfy's Hot Dog on a Fork guy is (35 feet large to be exact), and he is mighty shiny in spots. But then you notice–he doesn't have any arms and, well, he only has one leg, and that's only if you consider the handle on a fork a leg. In the pre-match staredown, Big Chief sets his ice-cold eyes on the Wolfy's Hot Dog on a Fork and the Wolfy's mascot starts to sweat bullets. Big Chief doesn't even take his glasses off for this match. As the bell goes off, Wolfy's Hot Dog on a Fork moves in tighter, bouncing forward like a kid on a pogo stick. Big Chief quickly slides to the ground for a leg sweep. Down goes the Hot Dog on a Fork. Big Chief then ends the bout by pulling the fork out of the dog and placing the fork into his back pocket for use at a South Side cookout later that night.

Winner: **Big Chief** by Fork removal - 15 seconds into the 1st round.

Heavyweight Championship
of the Fiberglass Hot Dog Mascot World:

The Gemini Giant vs Big Chief

There is a mutual respect between these two giants. Big Chief even removes his glasses for this match. As expected, this bout goes the full three rounds with plenty of contact. Chief survives a couple of rocket slaps to the head from G Squared, but at the close of the 3rd and final round, he takes the green machine down with another leg sweep and then follows with an elbow smash and an arm bar which leaves the Gemini Giant howling at the moon when the final bell rings. Outstanding match with plenty of action. But hey, when it comes down to it, Big Chief simply outlasted the Gemini Giant. I mean, people have been shooting Big Chief in the back with arrows for over 50 years and the guy hasn't even flinched yet. Talk about toughness. He's got it.

Winner by split decision – and Heavyweight Champion of the Fiberglass Hot Dog Mascot World: **Big Chief**.

The Hot Dog Quiz

1. Who claims to have invented the chili cheese dog?

2. Fat Tommy's serves up a Polish sausage wrapped in bacon and then deep fried and smothered in mustard, grilled onions and cheese. What is this creation called?

3. What fiberglass giant stands at the corner of 63rd and Pulaski and has been known to "sport his wares" from time to time?

4. On what South Side Street can you find three breweries within a thirty block stretch? And name them?

5. As a youngster, this hot dog fanatic once had the goal of running for mayor of Chicago. Who is this crazed person?

6. What does Kayleigh the Crab like to do with her pet crab?

7. Tony the Hat has been known to knock down a dog at the Wiener Circle. Where else might you find his likeness?

8. How many musical instruments does Kev the Keys play? Hint: it's the same number of ingredients that go atop the Chicago dog

9. At what Uptown dog joint can you find a tired dog taking a nap atop a fiberglass blue couch?

10. The dog owner from this dog joint offered his dogs at a picnic on the White House lawn at the request of President Obama?

11. What chef gave his restaurant the same name as the restaurant his great grandmother ran in the depression?

12. Where in Chicago you can you find five top-notch Italian restaurants in a two block radius?

13. The dogs at this place are good enough but it's the shrimp that is truly top-notch. Where?

14. If the current POTUS came to Chicago to get a hot dog, where would he likely NOT go?

15. At what dog joint/sandwich shop is the lady who runs the counter known as, Mama?

   **Answers on the following page

Answers

1. Fat Johnnie. (See page 57)
2. The Ditka (Long live Da Coach, See page 10)
3. Big Chief. (See page 43)
4. Western Avenue. Horse Thief Hollow, Open Outcry Brewing Co, and The Blue Island Beer Co (See page 89)
5. Dennis Foley. Source: my brain
6. Take it for a walk. (See page 59)
7. At Juvy hall and the FBI Building. (See page 61)
8. Seven. (See page 80)
9. Jake's Pup in the Ruf. (See page 8)
10. Byron's. (See page 78)
11. The Duck Inn, Kevin Hickey. (See page 40)
12. 24th and Oakley, Heart of Chicago. (See page 52)
13. 35th Street Red Hots. (See page 15)
14. Wiener Circle where the 3-inch Trump dog is a specialty. Source: the Wiener Circle sign (See page 36)
15. Branko's Sandwich Shop. (See page 46)

Henry's Drive In
6031 Ogden, Cicero
708-656-9344

Rating:

So let's just say I know a guy who wishes to go unnamed (let's just call him Tommy the Penguin, for kicks) who sent me a note to try the hot dog at Henry's. Well, I went, I saw, and I THOROUGHLY enjoyed. The Penguin was big-time correct on this dog recommendation.

The Henry's dog ($3.79 with fries) is not a Vienna Beef, David Berg or Red Hot Chicago dog. Rather, this dog has its own recipe, and I must say there is something noticeably different about the taste of the dog itself. And I mean that in an extremely positive way. It is DAMN tasty and comes dressed with mustard, onion, sport peppers, and a big ass pickle. The Penguin just celebrated his eighth decade of munching dogs from Henry's by snagging twenty-six dogs (yep, that's right−26) in January of this year, and bringing his prized dogs home for the entire extended family to enjoy. Now that's my kinda guy−reckless with his food adventures.

The Lowdown
Henry's Drive In – a Cicero stronghold

Tony Rotolo, the long-time owner of Henry's on Route 66 in Cicero, is about as likable as a guy can be. A quick smile, hearty laugh and laidback personality are part of his persona. As a young buck, he drove a truck for a beer distributor before moving into the food game at age 24.

"I bought a Tastee Freeze on 26th Street in Berwyn in 1982," Tony says. "It needed a bunch of work but I fixed it up and got it going the right way. It's just called, 'The Freeze' now, and we concentrate on ice cream products."

Tony still runs The Freeze (open seasonally). He bought Henry's in 1990.

Henry's Drive In

"My dad was good friends with Bob Henry. Bob's father originally opened the stand in the '50s, but eventually Bob was looking to sell and he offered it to my dad. But my dad died before he could buy the place, so Bob asked me if I wanted to buy it. That was thirty years ago."

The locals rave about the hot dog at Henry's. Other big sellers include their chicken sandwich, Polish, chili and Italian Beef. On Route 66, Henry's also gets a good amount of visitors every year who are out touring one of our country's most beloved roads in search of yesteryear and Americana. Inside, the walls are dotted with framed photos of Henry's as it changed over the years. Through it all, the big neon Hot Dog sign out front has always been there–bearing the words, "It's a meal in itself."

So let's get the full scoop on that dog, to that 'meal in itself', the top seller at Henry's. What is it exactly that makes the Henry's dog so damn tasty? When I came to visit Tony, we talked for a bit at a booth, then he brought me into the kitchen to watch the hot dog show in action, before taking me into the basement to show me one of his favorite pieces of hot dog equipment–the steam generator. A large apparatus, it looks much like the standard furnace you'd find in your own home. With its piping and ductwork, seeing it also brought back memories of *Mike Mulligan and his Steam Shovel*, a beloved kids' book my sons could never get enough of.

"Most hot dog stands use steam tables to cook their dogs," Tony says. "The heat source provided can cook the dogs and keep them warm for awhile, but when they sit in the steamer for a long period of time, the hot dog loses a lot of its flavor and it can change colors and get rubbery." After showing me the steam generator in the basement, Tony brought me back upstairs so I could see it in action. And I must say that this bad boy has some definite kick to it.

"This steam generator lets us cook a hot dog in a matter of seconds," Tony said. "That way, we can keep the hot dogs fresh and put them in as we need them. So they aren't sitting around in the steam table for long. The dog keeps more of its flavor that way and it always stays fresh."

Saying that the Henry's dog is tasty and fresh is a supreme understatement. Not only does the steam generator make sure the Henry's dog is always fresh, but add to it the wonderful, time-tested recipe Tony has put together to give his dog a unique taste. Henry's hot dogs are made pursuant to Tony's recipe by a food manufacturer in the far reaches of Michigan.

"I've tried to use some local places over the years to put the dog together using our recipe. Some did a good job but went out of business, and some couldn't consistently produce the dog the way I wanted it. But I'm happy with our current place. They do a great job. They follow our recipe to the T and when you add that to the flavor the dogs keep by not sitting in a steamer all day, it gives our customers a good dog."

There you have it—words of wisdom from a man who makes one of the Top Dogs in the Chicago area. And sure Tony has been at the helm for thirty years now, but he doesn't claim all the glory. Like the team player he is, he also passes out kudos to a number of long-time workers on his staff.

"We have a number of employees here now at Henry's," Tony says. "My mom and sister (Sue) helped here for a long time. My mom still helps now with the paperwork, and Sue still helps some too."

Add to that list All-Star employees like Carrie, Mary, and April, and you have a combined near ninety years of staff help.

"Both of my daughters worked here, too," says Mary, including one daughter who pitched in for eight years.

"This is definitely a neighborhood place," Carrie adds. "One generation brings in the next generation as customers and, sometimes, to work here too." Carrie laughs. "And we have sort of a Vegas theme here. What happens at Henry's stays at Henry's."

Oh, I'm sure that stories could be told about the colorful cast of characters who have bought a dog or worked at Henry's over the years. So stop in and say hello to the gang (they're a fun group) one day at Henry's and order up a couple of dogs. They are Top-Notch. For sure. And don't be surprised if you run into the ghost of Al Capone lurking near the building. Big Al used to frequent a house of ill repute just down the street back in his day.

Mustard's Last Stand
1613 Central, Evanston
847-864-2700

Rating:

From the red roof, to the white exterior walls, to the red trim, I love the look of this stand, set just a few football tosses from Ryan Field, Northwestern's football stadium. Get yourself a tasty Pinky ($3.59) with all of the M7s and snag a stool along the window counter. Munch on that dog and let your eyes roam the walls and take in all of the historical photos and paraphernalia that they have to offer. This place opened in the late '60s and screams OLD SCHOOL.

Jimmy's Red Hots
4000 W Grand, Chicago
773-384-9513   Rating:

Make no mistake about it, Jimmy's kicks out a great dog with plenty of snap. Everything here means mustard, onions, relish and peppers. Served with fresh cut fries for $3.26, this place is a bargain. This Vienna Beef Hall of Famer has been around since 1954. Stop in and grab a dog. The throwback experience is well worth it. You can bank on it.

Morrie O'Malley's Hot Dogs
3501 S Union, Chicago
773-247-2700   Rating:

During my days as a Streets and San guy, O'Malley's was one of my obligatory hot spots if my belly felt a little neglected as we neared the end of the workday. Our garage was just a mile away and a quick stop to O'Malley's on the way to the garage was always well worth it. Ah yes, there's nothing quite like a dog and a chocolate shake after a semi-hard, summer day of work.

The dog here is a beauty (a Thummy for $3) and in addition to the M7s, they toss a cucumber wedge into the mix, too. Yeah, baby, yeah. You'll never have to worry about these guys skimping. A Vienna Beef Hall of

Famer, Morrie O'Malley ran this place for nearly 40 years, starting out in a corner trailer before building the brick and mortar stand. New owner Sal Pappalito took over the reins a few years ago and I'm happy to say, everything is still top shelf. And hey, this is White sox country here, so if you happen to be a Cubbie fan, leave the blue at home. Trust me on that.

Around the corner

The home of Chicago political royalty is just a hop, skip, and a jump away. The Daley family's former home (as in King Richard I and King Richard II) is at 3536 S Lowe. This modest home is worthy of a look. Oh, if the walls could talk.

Byron's Hot Dogs
1017 W Irving Park, Chicago
773-281-7474   Rating:

When I think of a hot dog joint, I think of places like Byron's on Irving Park. This tiny box of a building (roughly 25 feet by 12 feet) is brightly colored and the entire west wall is covered with the Vienna Beef dog artwork. At Byron's, you can sit out on one of the picnic benches, stare at the Cubs logo emblazoned on the nearby storage shed, and knock down your dog as the Red Line L rattles past the Sheridan stop. This is Chicago at its finest, people.

And the phrase, "Drag it through the garden" applies in a HUGE way to the dogs ($3.75 for a Pinky) at Byron's where, in addition to the standard M7 ingredients, you can also get cucumber, green peppers, round pickles (in addition to the dill pickle) and lettuce atop that wiener. And believe me when I say this: the folks at Byron's don't hold back on those ingredients. You will have a virtual salad atop your dog when you walk out the door.

Though I'm a hot dog purist, at Byron's I still get loads of everything (but not lettuce—I still can't get myself to do that) on my dog. And then I pull some of the ingredients off and eat it as a side. Scrumdillicious. If you are a person with a big-time appetite, give the Dogzilla a try. This half-pound dog with all the trimmings ($6.63) can feed a family of four. Guaranteed. **Other location**: 1701 W Lawrence, Chicago.

The Lowdown
Byron's - The Straight Shooter

Byron's owner Mike Payne has been a frontrunner in Chicago's hot dog game for 45 years. He's opened new businesses and seen some succeed and some fail, he's shaken the hand of a U.S. president, and had his hot dogs devoured by members of the Cubs. Through those highs and lows, Mike has always been himself—a guy who tells it as he sees it.

"I worked for Tast-e Hast-e when I was a teenager," Mike says, referencing one of Chicago's now defunct beloved dog joints. "After that, I was a milk delivery man. That's how I met Byron. I was 19 and I used to deliver milk to his restaurant, The Lunch Pail. And Byron always wanted to open a hot dog stand, and I helped him do it and then helped run it. We opened up the stand on Irving Park in 1975."

Byron's Hot Dogs on Irving

Byron's opened its second location on Lawrence in 1983. "Those two places have done well through the years. Always." Borrowing the ultimate drag-it-through-the-garden ingredients from Taste-e Haste-e, where the M7 ingredients were expanded to include both pickle and cucumber, as well as lettuce and sliced green pepper, Byron's has succeeded by building a virtual salad atop your dog.

"I bought out Byron in 2006. He was sick and not doing well and wanted out of things. He died just a few years later (2012). We had expanded and added a couple of different locations over the years and we got stuck with a couple of rough deals. Quite frankly, around 2007-08, we were on the verge of bankruptcy. We lost the opportunity to get in at a great location, and our lease at our Forest Park location was killing us. Things weren't looking good."

Right about that time, President Obama's people contracted Mike to ask him to come to D.C. to serve hot dogs at a White House picnic, shortly after being elected president.

"When I got the call, I just figured it was a prank. But then I got follow up emails that had the official White House email on it. It was crazy."

Mike and his wife, Ann, flew out to D.C. "It was really cool. The White House staff people re-created my steam table and serving center based on some photos I sent to them." Mike felt at home serving folks at the picnic. "Ann and I had our photos taken with President Obama and I shook his hand. I'll never forget all that."

Following that exposure, Byron's quickly jumped back into the winner's circle. "People were flowing into our locations. And I was able to kill off that Forest Park lease after three years (rather than the full 10 years). That was a huge weight off of our shoulders. And things took off again."

"We've always offered quality products. Sure people know us for our hot dogs, but our hamburger with gyro meat and spices on it won the area Hamburger contest in 2018. And folks love our Dogzilla too (the ½ lb hotdog)."

The Byron's catering business is also on the move. "We had fun doing street fests. And after that we started getting invited to do birthday parties and corporate outings. It's good to see that happen, especially when we were close to folding up the tent not long ago."

Sure Mike runs the show at both Byron's locations but he's had some steady help over the years from long-time employees, as well as his wife.

"My wife handles the books for me," says Mike. "And I have some people who have worked for me for years and years."

Byron's has approximately twenty-eight employees in various capacities at the two restaurants. "We used to be part of a program called WECEP (Work Experience and Career Exploration Program) that was affiliated with the Chicago Public Schools where we would bring in young kids and have them work for us." A number of people still working for Byron's came in through that program. "Javier Barrera is one of my managers. Hard worker. He's 44 now but he started with us at sixteen. He came in through the program."

61-year-old Brant Lidman is another of those long-time employees. He's been with Byron's since he was 15. As I was leaving the Byron's on Lawrence, Brant was working the counter. I asked him how Mike has changed over the years.

"Mike's calmed down a bunch with time," Brant says, tossing a playful jab Mike's way. "He's much more mellow now."

So what's next for Byron's? "We might be opening a third location. We've done our scouting and are getting close to pulling the trigger. But we'll wait and see what happens." The words of a straight shooter.

Flub a Dub Chubs

3021 N Broadway, Chicago

773-857-6500   Rating:

I absolutely love the feel of this subterranean dog joint. Here in the down under, you'll find a number of great dogs to choose from and the ketchup wall of shame to go with it. My kinda place.

I upped my game here and went with the signature Chubby ($9 with fries) This ¼ pound bad boy is a definite stomach pleaser with all of the M7s intact. Yummy. This place refuses to put ketchup on a dog, and I absolutely love that. But Rosemary (one of the owners) does leave a tub of ketchup on the counter, should you wish to apply your own. But be prepared to pay the price: if Rosemary or one of the other workers happens to see you committing this sad act, they will slide out from behind the counter, snap your photo on an instamatic, and slap it on the Ketchup Wall of Shame. Nice to see that Moses' 11th commandment, "Thou shall never place ketchup on a Chicago Dog," is being followed here.

Consigliere No. 3

Hot Tip from Kev the Keys

A hot dog fanatic, 35-year-old Kev the Keys is a mover and shaker who also happens to play seven musical instruments. That's right, seven. That's all the toes on one foot plus a couple from the other. Kev the Keys can play the hell out of most any instrument, but don't ask him to sing. Absolutely not. His microphone voice has been known to make sober people fall off of bar stools and cause drunks to sprint blindly out the tavern doors into traffic. Kev the Keys prefers to stay silent and bang the ivories of his instrument of choice—any keyboard. And when he's not working at UIC, he's out doing one of two things: gigging with his band at various North Side locations or eating hot dogs.

"I absolutely love the Chicago style hot dog. It's my definite favorite," Kev says, "but for something different, I like to pop into Flub a Dub Chubs."

Sure this place offers the classic Chicago dog (the Flubby), but the other dogs, according to Kev the Keys, are mighty tasty, too. "You can't go wrong with any of the specialty dogs but my two favorites are the Chihuahua and the BLT dog."

The Chihuahua ($11 with fries) is a basic Chicago dog topped with bacon, avocado, pico and sour cream. Brothers and sisters, if that doesn't make you start foaming at the mouth, nothing will. But it's the BLT dog ($8 with fries) that is Kev's true favorite.

"This is a bacon-wrapped char dog with mayo, a thin bed of lettuce and some tomato slices. Excellent. And the mayo is a nice touch. Overall, it's simple and kind of light. You'll love it."

Words of wisdom from Kev the Keys. Mark 'em down, folks. And if you happen to run into Kev at a dog joint or a bar gig one night, ask him about some of his other favorite dog joints. He's got plenty. Just don't ask him to sing.

Duk's Red Hots

636 N Ashland, Chicago

312-733-0069   Rating:

    This cool old shack is the original in what at one time was over a dozen Duk's dog stands locally. The candy cane red and white striping gives this building and outdoor seating area a definite feel of years gone by. And this delicious dog (a Pinky with all the M7s sans tomatoes) has plenty of snap and comes with fries for $3.75. Grab a seat at the counter and fire a few questions at the gal working the grill. She'll fill you up with some of the history on the place, the movies filmed there, and the big shots who have waltzed through the door. Good stuff.

Fred and Jack's

7600 S Yale, Chicago

773-783-9700   Rating:

    Though the original owners are long gone, this stand has stood the test of time at the corner of 76th and Vincennes for well over 50 years. You are in the heart of the South Side here and Fred and Jack's kicks out a whopper of a dog (1/4 pounder with fresh cut fries for $3.75). It's mighty big and mighty tasty. But take note: a dog with everything comes with mustard, onions, gigantic peppers, round pickles, lettuce and Ketchup. That's right, KETCHUP. I was about to call in the hot dog police to investigate when I noticed the red splash on my dog. Instead I went in to see the manager and this is what he said, "We wanted to do something a little different so instead of tomatoes, we went with lettuce and ketchup." The guy probably puts ketchup on his steak, too. But I digress: this big ass dog with fries is a great bang for your buck.

Dan's Hot Dogs
9314 S Ashland, Chicago
773-779-9123

Rating:

This dog (a Thummy for $2.39) is always full of snap and the M7s are fresh as fresh can be. Toss the fresh cut fries into the mix and you're all set. The folks at Dan's are friendly and the colorful shack gives off that same feel. Grab a seat at a picnic table just outside the door and tear into that dog. It is one of the best in the city and I asure you, you will enjoy it.

The burgers ($3.99) here are homemade with seasoning that will cause your taste buds to do somersaults of joy. This place also has a solid chili ($3.20 for a Large), guaranteed to warm your inners on a cold winter day.

The Lowdown

Dan's Hot Dogs - Movin' On Up

Tom Theodorou, co-owner of Dan's Hot Dogs, has a story he likes to tell.

"In the mid-70s, I used to walk from where I lived in Cicero to go to work at the Seneca restaurant in Berwyn," Tom starts. "I was fourteen then and it was about four miles each way. That's just how it was back then. Along the way, I used to stop at a hardware store and peek through the window at this new bike they had in there. Every few days, I'd stop and look. The store owner came outside one day to talk to me. I'm sure he saw me looking at the bike before. I still didn't speak much English then but I knew some. He asked me if I would like the bike. I let him know that I did not have any money. He asked if I had a job and I told him that I did. I told him I was a bus boy at Seneca. He told me that I could take the bike and stop by and pay $10 towards the bike each week. And if I didn't have $10, I could pay $5 until it was paid off." Tom smiles. "What a nice man. After that I rode my bike to and from work every day and everywhere else."

Not a bad introduction to the Windy City area for young Tom, who left his hometown of Scala, Greece to come to Chicago at age 14. "I was just a kid when I came here. I didn't know the language. It was cold. I had never seen snow before and it was everywhere." Tom laughs. "In school I didn't do well in anything but gym." A wrestler in Greece, Tom found a place where he belonged on his high school wrestling team. "That really kept me going. It let me have some fun."

Tom worked for five years at Seneca Restaurant, starting with that bus boy position before becoming a dishwasher. After that, he became a cook. The Seneca owners were good to him. "They gave me steady work. They gave me the chance to move up to better jobs. It's funny, but early on, after I became a dishwasher, the cooks would let me come in and work at the grill every so often. They showed me some things. The owners didn't know about this. And then one day, the cooks didn't show up to work. Who knows what happened? The owner was panicking. I told him I could cook. He didn't believe me, but I went into that kitchen and started cooking, and the owner saw me. He watched me and then he said, 'Yeah, I guess you can cook.'"

Dan's Dogs

Tom worked as a cook at a number of restaurants over the years before he and his wife Danila bought Dan's in

1999, about a decade after they were married. "My wife is from Columbia and when it comes to running things at Dan's, she's definitely the boss."

At first they sold a few staple products—primarily hot dogs and Polish sausages. Over the years they added a grill and deep fryer. "And we make our hamburgers fresh daily. I run it through the grinder and add my spices," says Tom.

"The hot dog and Polish are still our best seller's today," but he adds, "people like our burgers and our chicken breast sandwiches too. And we go through a lot of chili."

Tom shows pride as he mentions that Mayor Richard M. Daley used to stop by Dan's every so often when he was the man in the big car. "Sometimes he would come by with his guard, and sometimes he would send someone out to get the hot dogs to bring back."

Likeable and self-effacing, there are no flies on Tom Theodorou. And when I think of him and his life's journey, I can't get the theme song—*Movin' on Up*—from the '70s and '80s sit com *The Jeffersons*, out of my head. It fits. And though Tom and Danila are not ready to retire just yet, there have been discussions. "We would like to travel more. Go places in the U.S. on our motorcycle. And travel to other countries. As far as settling down, I think maybe Florida. There's no snow there and I like to fish." Tom has certainly earned his piece of the pie.

Fast Track
629 W Lake, Chicago
312-993-9300

Rating:

M M M

This stand offers a solid pinky with all the M7s for $3.99. As you munch on your grub, you'll hear the roar of the Green Line L as it rolls down Lake Street. The owner is a funny guy. When I went to pay for my dog, he asked if I wanted any fries or a drink. When I declined, he said, in typical Chicago fashion, "How am I supposed to make any money?" This West Loop spot offers breakfast too.

Bob O's Hot Dogs
8258 W Irving Park, Chicago
773-625-9840

Rating:

M M M 1/2

Since the '50s, Bob-O's has been a mainstay on the Northwest Side. This Pinky is excellent with all of the M7s and comes with a boatload of fresh cuts fries for $3.75. If your stomach is screaming, "Where's the beef?" this is an excellent place to have at it. The Italian beef is tasty and done just right. Grab a seat at one of the stools along the window and dig in. You'll like it. Oh yeah.

Janson's Drive In
9900 S Western, Chicago
773-941-6283   Rating:

This nostalgic throwback has been a family favorite
for decades for many in the Beverly area. First opened in
1960, the Janson family served Oscar Mayer all-beef
dogs, and they were mighty tasty. Since 2014, the new
owners have been doing a great job running the show and
made the switch to Vienna Beef products. This steamed
the buns of a few locals, but all I have to say is: C'mon,
people. It's Vienna Damn Beef. It doesn't get any better
than that. The dog here is a Thummy ($2.89) and it's
rock solid and made with all of the M7 fresh ingredients.
The menu now includes such items as the Angus beef
burger ($5.25 for 1/3 pounder) and the grilled, wild-
caught Sockeye Salmon sandwich ($10.89), served on
focaccia bread with lettuce, tomato, arugula, red onion,
Chipotle aioli sauce, and then finished with a lemon
vinaigrette. Wow. If that doesn't make your mouth
water, you're likely ready for the grave. And make sure
you get a Janson's banana shake ($3.85), made with
actual bananas (imagine that), before you leave. You can
thank me later.

Around the corner

You're in my stomping grounds
here, as well as the home of the
South Side St. Patrick's Day
Parade. On Western, from 99th
Street to 113th Street, you'll find over a dozen pubs,

including two great breweries, all on the west side of the street (the east side is dry). My suggestion: After you down your lunch dog and banana shake at Janson's, head to **Horse Thief Hollow** (10428 S Western) for a quality craft beer or two (the Kitchen Sink is my favorite), and then meander a few more blocks down the road to **Open Outcry Brewing Company** (10934 S Western) for a few more excellent craft beers (the hazy, New England IPA is my Go To here). The final touch: you're just a few blocks from **Joey's Red Hots** at 115th and Western, so you can snag that dinner dog you've no doubt been craving. And don't forget the fries. You'll need something to soak up all those bevvies you just drank, you lush. If you're in the mood for a dessert beer, the **Blue Island Beer Company** is on Western, as well (13357 S Old Western, Blue Island, to be exact). This hip tap room offers some solid craft bevvies—including one that carries my favorite name for a local craft beer—Massive Political Corruption. Now that's a full day.

Nicky V's (formerly Doug's Dogs)
6200 W 159th Street, Oak Forest
708-687-1122   Rating:

MMM1/2

First things first: How can you not like a hot dog shack with Lady Liberty on the roof? You can't. But here's the deal, Lady Liberty or not, I'm not coming back if the dog isn't any good. Not a problem at Nicky V's. Whenever I venture into Oak Forest for a youth lacrosse game or if I have to battle my way through the traffic and malls in Orland Park on my way to visit my brother, I always make a stop at Nicky V's on the way back. The dog (a skinless Thummy) is mighty tasty and priced right at $2.80 with yummy fresh cut fries. On a nice day, grab a table out front and watch the traffic zip past as you munch on one of the best dogs in the Southwest burbs.

The Lowdown

Nicky V's - The New Kid on the Block

As you cruise towards Nicky V's on 159th Street, the first thing you'll likely notice as you get closer is the eight foot tall replica of the Statue of Liberty standing erect upon the roof, her right arm bearing the torch and reaching high into the sky to welcome the huddled masses to a top-notch dog at Nicky V's.

"She's been stolen from the roof a few times over the years," says owner Nick Versetto with a laugh. "I guess it was a senior prank for some of the local high school kids."

Though he's 37 years old, at first glance, Nick looks like he could fit in with that high school crowd. But his pranking days are over.

"I bought the business and the building just over two months ago (October of 2019)," Nick says. 'This place has been here since the late '70s. At first it was a Jr's, and then Doug bought it in 1991. It changed hands a few more times. And now that I own it, I want to put my mark on it." That includes a name change to Nicky V's.

An affable guy with a quick smile, Nick shares a bit of his past. "I did pretty well in high school and had opportunities to go to some nice colleges, but my parents got divorced. And basically, they told me that college was going to be on me." Nick laughs. "I didn't want to carry that debt so I started working instead."

Nicky V's

Over the years Nick has worked primarily in the banking industry. He has also rehabbed and flipped some houses. But through it all, in the back of his mind, he always held onto the notion of owning a hot dog stand or fast food place one day.

"I always wanted to own a place like this," Nick says.

"And now, I'm really enjoying meeting the customers and getting a chance to know them. This is a nice location. Lots of good people around here. And it's great when I get positive feedback from customers about the food. When they say how much they like it, it makes you feel good."

I sit on a chair inside Nicky V's a few days after Christmas and watch Nick and one other employee work the lunch crowd. The place is jumping as Nick and Jose work together making dogs, fresh cut fries and filling other orders. Nick talks in spurts while working the register and filling the orders.

"My wife Krystyna and I share the hours here. I still work in the banking industry and then put in my hours here. We've only been here for two months now so we're still learning. But we love it."

One of the very first things Nick did was change suppliers. "We went back to Vienna beef products," Nick says. "I wanted the best for my customers." Nick also adjusted the pricing on the menu. "Quite frankly, the last owner had some meal prices that were way too high. I dropped the pricing on our meals to make it more affordable. And I think that will lead to more volume as well. I also switched to fresh cut fries which I feel are the best. I want people to see and taste the quality."

The hot dog is definitely the top seller on the menu. As the lunch crowd rolls in and out, Nick talks and jokes with his customers—almost all of whom order a dog, a Polish, or the jumbo dog. A few chicken pita orders come in, along with a Philly cheese steak, but the dog is definitely king. "It's only $2.80 for a hot dog with fresh cut fries," Nick says. "We're selling a bunch." And they should. After all, hot dog fans love a good deal. And this

$2.80 dog with fresh cut fries is definitely that–a quality dog at a good price. And Nick is all about quality and fair pricing. Cheers to the new kid on the block.

Express Grill
1260 S Union, Chicago
312-738-2112   Rating:

Sure I like Maxwell Street dogs but not nearly as much as the classic Chicago dog. And though I can never get enough grilled onions, I still prefer the classic. That being said, Express serves a nice dog ($4.25 with fries). 'Everything' comes with mustard, a mound of lovely grilled onions, and relish (along with two big ass peppers wrapped on the side). Most Maxwell Street Polish/Dog joints don't toss relish into the mix. I rather like the addition. The relish gave the dog a bit more pop. Damn Tasty for sure. And this is always a great place for a late night snack. Open 24 hours.

Jim's Original
1250 S Union, Chicago
312-733-7820   Rating:

This is where the Maxwell Street Polish started. Hence the word 'Original'. This Thummy ($4.25 with fries) is served with mustard, grilled onions, and peppers on the side. It had been awhile since I scored a Jim's Original dog and it did not disappoint. The line was long but moved quick and the traffic along the Dan Ryan was music to my ears. Open 24 hours.

DARE TO COMPARE – Dogs only
Express Grill vs Jim's Original

Who doesn't like a good feud? I certainly do. And when a feud goes on for decades and decades, it makes it all the more intriguing. So here they are . . . the Hatfields (Express Grill) and the McCoys (Jim's Original). Or maybe it's more akin to CVS vs. Walgreens, or Mickey Ds vs. Burger King, or better yet, The White Sox vs the Cubs. You get the picture. How in the heck can two, 24-hour hot dog/Polish/pork chop/hamburger huts not only exist shoulder to shoulder, but actually thrive? The answer is simple. They both kick out excellent products at reasonable prices.

Both Jim's and Express were originally established on Halsted Street, near Maxwell Street, but relocated around 2004 when UIC expanded. If you troll the Dan Ryan on a regular basis, you've no doubt seen both of these age-old gems standing on the west side of the road, alongside the Roosevelt Avenue entrance ramp. The buildings are separated only by a tiny parking lot. The original owners of Jim's and Express were related, and no doubt a few family hairs were ruffled when Express opened just down the street from Jim's in the 1950s.

All that being said, when it comes to the dogs, I was impressed with both. On this excursion, I first ate the

Express dog and fry and then had my Jim's Original dog and fry about 15 minutes after that. Not a bad way to spend a sunny, winter afternoon. As I noted in my review, I liked the relish on the Express dog. It went surprisingly well with the grilled onions. The Express dog also had a bit more snap to it, and I found this extremely odd as both Express and Jim's were both inducted into the Vienna Beef Hall of Fame in 2013. How could one dog have more snap when they both came from the same company? The answer was staring right at me.

As we all know, Vienna Beef is the overwhelming dog of choice for our local stands. Express's ties to Vienna Beef are noted all over its building, but the more I looked, I couldn't find any such signage at Jim's. In fact, I found that a Vienna Beef sign painted on the rear of the building had been whited-over. After a bit of additional sleuthing (a call to its corporate office – yes, Jim's has a corporate office and a telephone answering system that could rival any Fortune 500 company) revealed that Jim's had cut the Vienna Beef ties a few years ago and now has its hot dogs and Polish sausages made elsewhere pursuant to its own recipe.

So that accounts for what I perceived as Jim's lack of snap when compared to Express. Toss the relish into the mix, and things are looking good for Express. Lastly, the fresh cut fries at Express were better than Jim's fries. Winner in the Dare to Compare Dog category: Express Grill.

So there you have it. Hot dog sleuthing at its finest. My next sleuthing mission: to find the **Loch Ness Monster**. I hear he's in Lake Michigan now. Anyone see him lately?

Clark Street Dogs
3040 N Clark, Chicago
773-281-6690   Rating:

Whenever a quality dog shack is also attached to a bar, that's my kind of a place. Go snag a yummy dog (a Thummy with extremely fresh M7 ingredients for $3.82) and then wander into the pub for a cold bevvie. The dog is good, the beer is cold, and the conversation lively.

If you're planning to throw down a few beers, I suggest going with the Philly Cheese steak ($10.15) which is almost as good as the real McCoy out East, and it will sop up more of the beer. Before you waltz out the door, and only if you're feeling a wee bit adventurous, snag a Pickleback shot where you'll have the opportunity to savor this booze concoction tied in with Vienna Whole Spear pickle juice. I'm all about the pickle.

Portillo's
Everywhere and beyond
Rating:

As we all know, Portillo's has a kick ass dog done the right way with a Thummy topped with all the M7s. What Dick Portillo started in a tiny trailer, turned into a nationwide empire that he sold for a billion smackeroos in 2014. Sure you can get virtually any sort of food you want at Portillos, but just remember it all started with a hot dog and a dream.

Fatso's Last Stand
2258 W Chicago, Chicago
773-245-3287   Rating:

This stronghold in Ukranian Village is my GO TO when I'm feeling the need for a char dog. If you want a classic steamed dog, don't come to Fatso's. You will not find one here. And if you are in a hurry, you should ease on down the road as this wonderful dog takes about 10 minutes on the grill to get it where it needs to be. But if you're craving a char dog, and you have some time to spare, this sliced and blackened wiener (served with all of the M7s and fresh cut fries for $5.00) fills the bill. If you see a burger in your future, check out the huge Samuel's Double Fatso Extreme (a double burger with bacon and a fried egg, $10.00). It is a doozy.

Don's Drive In
7748 S Kedzie, Chicago
773-476-9392   Rating:

Don's has a great hot dog shack look to it, with colors galore, and complete with Mr. Hot Dog himself standing atop the building (see photo on Page 5). One of my long time favorites, the dog here is a Pinky ($2.78) with all of the M7 fixins and plenty of SNAP. And the fries here are always melt-in-your-mouth good. Be sure to get an order. If you feel the need for something else, try the Italian beef ($6.06), always a steady gamer. The dog here is one of the best on the South Side.

Chubby Wieners
4652 N Western, Chicago
773-775-7600   Rating:

Just a few steps from the Brown Line stop at Western, the Chicago dog is top-notch (a Pinky for $3.25) and comes with all of the M7s. Fresh, fresh, fresh. If you'd like to up your game, go for the 7-inch, signature Famous Chubby Wiener. But the Fourkas brothers are also known for their specialty dog creations. Of these, the Senor Gordo (a deep-fried Chubby Wiener wrapped in bacon and topped with Jalapeno mustard, pico de gallo, and jalapenos - $8.99) is my favorite. Come one, come all to the Chubby Wiener. You will not be disappointed.

The Lowdown
Chubby Wieners – Out to Conquer the Hot Dog World

In the mid-1990's, cartoon characters Pinky and the

Brain had a master plain–TO TAKE OVER THE WORLD. Each episode ended in failure as the self-centered Brain's plans were always shattered, usually undone by his pal, the good-natured but feeble minded, Pinky. Fast forward to 2005, and enter: The Fourkas brothers–Taso, then 25, and Anthony, then 20. They too developed a master plan–"TO BECOME THE GREAT-EST HOT DOG STAND THE WORLD HAS EVER KNOWN." Unlike the cartoon characters, however, the Fourkas brothers' master plan has been anything but a failure. Rather, the brothers' Lincoln Square stand is thriving and growing.

"Our beloved Uncle Chub had one last wish before he passed away," says Anthony, now 35, "and that wish was to open a hot dog stand. [That's how] Chubby Wieners was born."

So there you have it. With all of the great dog stands in Chicago, to become the GREATEST dog stand the world has ever known is a mighty big goal. But, hey, why not aim for the top.

While the classic Chicago dog and the Chubby Wiener (a bigger Chicago dog) are definite winners, the specialty dogs at Chubby Wieners keep the locals coming back for more.

"The specialty dogs were first created for the Chubby Wieners food truck, our company's Hunger Fighting Machine. We wanted to give the customers something special, an explosion of flavors in their mouths."

What followed from there was a number of Pinky and the Brain-like experiments, but in the kitchen, where the

Fourkas brothers explored different ingredient combinations over and over again. The result: a number of award-winning creations that will make your taste buds do a happy dance.

Chubby Wieners

"The Momona received Food Network's "Best in Show," says Anthony about the award accepted at Food Network's Concert at the Ravinia in 2014. "The Momona has sweet notes for the everyone's palate as you combine a famous Chubby Wiener lined with our applewood smoked bacon, topped with caramelized pineapples, blue cheese crumbles, and drizzled with our in-house citrus bbq sauce" If your mouth isn't watering now, slap yourself.

Okay, Brain, or I mean, Anthony, tell us about another specialty dog.

"The Senor Gordo was awarded "Chicago's Best" and is known for its kick," says Anthony. "It's a Famous Chubby Wiener wrapped in bacon and deep fried. It's topped with our house made jalapeno mustard, lime-cut Pico de gallo, and fresh jalapeno. We bring the heat, in a good way." And if your mouth still isn't watering, slap yourself twice. Just cuz.

My suggestion: stop in, order up your dog, and listen to the rattle of the nearby L train as you munch. The Fourkas brothers have a good thing going here. No doubt, Uncle Chub would be proud.

Around the corner

Just a few feet away from the Fourkas wiener fort, you'll find the **Leland Tap** 4662 N Western). Any bar with an Old Style sign still swinging over the doorway is always worthy of a gander. Pop in and get yourself a bevvie to wash that dog down. And if you go there after Chubby Wieners is closed, you may find Anthony Fourkas sitting on a stool. The old and glorious **Davis Theater** (4614 N Lincoln) is one of the few remaining neighborhood theatres in the city. Built near the end of WWI, this theatre is truly worthy of its landmark status and a great place to check out a flick.

Devil Dawgs
2147 N Sheffield, Chicago
773-281-4300   Rating:

MMM1/2

Devil Dawgs jumped into the hot dog world in 2010 at this location and has since added two others. This tasty dog (A Pinky with all of the M7s for $3.50) is oh-so good, the fresh cut fries are solid, and the stand itself gives off a cool vibe.

When the iconic dog shack, Demon Dogs, was closed by the city in 2003 to allow for renovations at the Fullerton Red Line stop, Lincoln Parkers lost a favorite. Devil Dawgs has certainly helped fill the void. **Other locations:** 767 S State; 1431 N Milwaukee; and 937 W Belmont.

Gene and Jude's
2720 N River Road, River Grove
773-296-1500   Rating:

MMM1/2

This historic icon has been churning out dogs at this location since the '50s, though the original stand was opened at Polk and Western in the mid-40s. As Gene and Jude's proudly boasts, this place has "No seats, No ketchup, No pretense, No nonsense." It is all of that and more, and has won awards on top of awards.

The dog ($3.20 comes depression style—with mustard, onions, relish and sport peppers), has plenty of snap and comes with a heaping of fries tossed atop it. Jump in line and order your dog. It will come your way with quick, assembly line efficiency.

Chicago's Dog House
816 W Fullerton, Chicago
773-248-3647   Rating:

My cousins Jake and Elwood Blues will fix their eyes upon you from their spot on the wall when you push through the door to this cozy, shoebox stand. I love the inners of this place. It screams homey and cool. This Pinky ($3.80) is tasty and has all the M7s on it. But most folks come here to get the specialty dogs and sausages. Of these, the Midway Monster (a dog topped with bacon, giardiniera, cheddar cheese and BBQ sauce; $5.50) is my favorite.

Consigliere No. 4

Hot Tip from Sunshine Aime

I call her Sunshine Aime because she always has a smile on her face and she never fails to have something good to say about someone. But that being said, Sunshine Aime is no push over when it comes to THE CHICAGO DOG, or any relatives thereof.

"The traditional Chicago red hot at the Dog House has great snap. Truly a classic." Not a bad way to start the show, Sunshine Aime. What else ya got?

"The BLT dog is really light and refreshing and has great crunch. From the crispy bacon bits (rather than the hot dog being wrapped in bacon) to the great snap as well."

Okay, Sunshine Aime, I like what you're saying. Tell me more. Any big–time specialty dogs that make your mouth water?

"Try the Apple Brandy Duck sausage," says Amie. "This one is my absolute favorite. It has great sweetness from the sausage and caramelized onions. And yet the savoriness from the cheese and mustard cannot be overstated. A great balance."

Wow, I'm ready to head out for an Apple Brandy Duck sausage. I mean, sausage and booze, what more could a South Side Irish guy ask for?

"You may also want to try the Alligator sausage. It's juicy and flavorful," says Sunshine Aime. "Great sweet-heat from the chili sauce. Top it off with some caramelized onions and this is truly delicious."

Such a quandary. And yet Sunshine Aime has a bit more to say. "And don't forget to try the 'frips,' a cross between fries and chips. A MUST if you go there."

Thanks, Sunshine Amie. You hit the proverbial nail on the head.

Budacki's Drive In
4739 N Damen, Chicago
773-561-1322

Rating:

MMMM

Budacki's has been one of my North Side Go To joints for years. The building itself has a classic hotdog stand look. The barn red exterior walls with a touch of yellow and a hint of blue definitely does the magic. Pull into the side lot and step inside for a tasty dog (a Pinky with all of the M7s and fries for $3.50). Slide into a stool along the window or in one of the booths and enjoy the hell out of that dog. And you won't ever have to worry about slip sliding away on one of those stools. Each stool leg has a tennis ball attached to its bottom to prevent such slippage. Now that's Chicago, baby. Cash only.

The Lowdown
Budacki's Drive In – Good Neighbors

Bruno "Bud" Budacki and his wife Marge first opened up this picturesque stand just off of the corner of Damen and Lawrence in the early 1960s. Back then, it was all about the hot dogs. As the years moved on, Bud added items to the menu and he also grew to become fast friends with Chan Lee and Yong Lee, his Korean business neighbors who ran an Asian restaurant just a few doors south on Damen. In the late '70s, at Bud's suggestion as he neared retirement, the Lees bought Bud and Marge out and eventually closed their other eatery to focus on Budacki's.

"My parents and the Budackis spent a lot of time together over the years," says Jae Lee, 49, son of Chan and Yong. "I always considered Bud to be like my godfather. And he built Budacki's himself, from the ground up." With his father, Jae now helps run Budacki's and has been involved in a big way at the restaurant for over twenty years.

"When I was a little kid, I always used to hang around Budacki's all the time," Jae says. "Bud still owned the place then and he used to have framed photos of rattle snakes on the walls. I thought that was cool. And he kept snakes in cages in an area at the back of the store."

Budacki's Drive In

After the Lees bought Budacki's Drive In, their friendship with Bud and Marge continued to grow. "My parents emigrated to this country in 1972. I was just two at the time. They were hard working people who thought you had to work, work, work. 7 days a week. If you took a day off, you might lose your customers. That's how they thought back then." Jae smiles. "It was Bud who taught my parents that it was okay to take a day off every week. That it was okay to take a vacation."

And so it was that on some of those days off and for

some of those vacations, the Lees would travel to Wisconsin to visit Bud and Marge who had a place up there.

"Coming from an urban setting, the place was completely different for me," Jae says. "There were fields and woods everywhere. And rivers. And there was only one store in town, called, 'The Store.' I loved going up there to stay with the Budackis. I always saw something different, and it was good for my parents to be there, too. To get a break."

After more than forty years of friendship, Bud passed away several years ago, as did Jae's mother, Yong. Cancer played a part in both of their deaths. "My mother fought cancer for thirteen years," Jae says. "She was the family matriarch and she relished that role."

Jae now splits time between Budacki's and Crisp, a Lakeview restaurant specializing in Korean fried chicken and more, run by Jae and his partners. Each day, Jae comes to Budacki's in the mornings to help prepare everything, before heading to Crisp most afternoons where he spends the balance of the workday.

"My dad is 83 now but he still comes to Budacki's every day," Jae says. "It's a definite part of him. For sure."

Over the years, Jae has made changes to the menu, some of which met with resistance from his loyal customers. "When we came out with the Veggie Dog, some customers were really turned off by it. That was six, seven years ago. Some people looked at it like it was an insult to serve a Veggie Dog in a hot dog stand. The two couldn't co-exist. Crazy stuff like that." With time, the Veggie Dog at Budacki's became a big seller on the menu and has now even been accepted by the Budacki loyalists. "But that's fine,' Jae says. "People need to voice their opinion. I respect that. I love the interaction with people, with the customers at both places,"

But the time Jae spends at Budacki's is something he cherishes. "My dad is here every day. And I get to work with him, to be with him." Something tells me, that Bud Budacki would like that.

The Plush Pup
5344 N Cumberland, Chicago
773-693-4311   Rating:

You will be at the far Northwest reaches of the city when you visit the Plush Pup, sitting at the end of a strip mall. The second you enter, you'll feel that 1950-ish diner vibe. Fun stuff. And the dog, this Thummy is a winner at $3.55 and comes with all of the M7s and with a cucumber wedge to boot. Oh yeah.

This joint has an extensive menu, so you can fill your belly with whatever you'd like. If you're feeling the ribs, go for it. For a fast food place, the ribs ($11.99 for half slab/$19.99 for a full) are rock solid.

Carm's Beef
1057 W Polk, Chicago
312-738-1046

Rating:

Carm's is located at one of my favorite fast food corners in Chicago. Just a few blocks off Taylor Street's main drag, it sits on the southwest corner of Polk and Carpenter and across the street is one of my primo sub joints, Fontanos. Carm's was my last stop on my mission of 50 dogs in 50 days, so I saved its place as the last spot in the book. And sure this place is known for its damn tasty Italian beef, but the dog here is also outstanding (with all the M7s sans tomato) and has plenty of snap. Owner Steve De Vivo is an affable guy and runs a top-notch food joint. Stop in, snag a dog, a beef or whatever you want (tacos, burgers, and more), and make sure you get an Italian ice if it's a hot summer day. Carm's has one of the absolute best ices in the city.

Around the corner

Sure you can get a great meal or a slice of Za at many of the Taylor Street eateries, but I suggest strolling just around the corner from Carm's to **Tufano's Vernon Park Tap** (1073 W Vernon Park Place, 312-733-3393), where you can get some mighty tasty Paisan food in a homey, no frills setting. I absolutely, positively love the water fountain in the square just outside of the restaurant. Tufano's is old school at its best and you won't break the bank here.

The TOPS

Top 5 South Side Hot Dogs.
1. Fat Johnnies
2. Don's Drive In on Kedzie
3. Fat Tommy's
4. Dan's Hot Dogs
5. The Skyway Dog House

Top 5 North Side Hot Dogs
1. Wolfy's
2. Byron's Hot Dogs
3. Superdawg
4. Branko's Sandwich Shop
5. Budacki's Drive In

Top 5 Suburban Hot Dogs
1. Henry's Drive In
2. The Launching Pad
3. Gene and Jude's
4. Mustard's Last Stand
5. Nicky V's

Top 5 Specialty Dogs
1. The Duck Inn
2. Kimski
3. Chubby Wieners
4. Flub a Dub Chubs
5. Hot G

50 Hot Dogs in 50 Days

Foley's Start Vitals: Height: 6'3" inches   Weight:231 pounds

Dec 9
Dan's
Fat Johnnies
Don's Drive In
Fat Tommy
Dec 12
Janson's
Skyway Dog House
Dec 14
Windy City Dogs
Parisi's Drive Inn
Jacky's
Dec 17
Doug's Dogs
Dec 18
The Launching Pad
Dec 20
O'Malley's
Express Grill
Jim's Original
Dino's Dogs
Dec 26
Quick Bite
Jake's Pup in the Ruf
Byron's
Dec 29
Susie's Drive Thru
Wolfy's Hot Dogs
Dec 30
Nathan's in Hyde Park
Jan 2
The Duck Inn
Chicago's Dog House
Dog House Grill

Jan 3
Don's in Orland
Snappy Dog
Superdawg
Chubby Wieners
Jan 5
Kimski
Jr's
Jan 7
Lu Lu's
Don's Famous Dogs
Martin's Corner
Jan 9
35th Street Red Hots
Henry's Drive In
Jan 11
The Duck Inn (again)
January 14
Flub a Dub Chubs
Brankos
Devil Dawgs
Clark Street Dogs
Wrigleyville Dogs
Jan 16
Budacki's
The Plush Pup
Gene and Jude's
Bob O's
Mr. D's Shish Kabob
Jan 19
Duk's
Fatso's Last Stand
Red Hot Ranch
Mustard's Last Stand

Jan 21
Joey's
Wiener Circle
Hot G
Jan 23
Fred & Jack's
Portillo's
Jan 24
Dave's Red Hots
Jimmy's Red Hots
Fast Tracks
Carm's
Total Stops
59
Total Dogs
60

Foley's End Vitals: Height: still 6'3" inches   Weight:233 pounds

Last Words

This was a wonderful journey of food and stories. I count myself lucky to have been able to hear the words of so many hard-working people. My blue-collar roots are part of my fabric and when I visited with the owners of these dog joints, I was visiting my own. I am proud to share their stories.

Each owner offered a part of themselves and with every story I heard, I became a better listener. Among other things, these mustard slappers shared stories about their youth, their aging parents, business decisions that went south, the death of a loved one, the difficulties you face in a new country, and the pros and cons of running a hot dog stand. We learn much when we listen to others. And so it was that with every story I heard, I'd like to think that I became a better person. Their stories are now a part of me. So, to all the mom and pop owners I interviewed, again I extend my thanks. You gave me your time and your words. Much appreciated.

And as for the Chicago dog itself, I ended up eating far more than 50 dogs to get my Top 50. I had my own list of favorites accumulated during years of roaming the city's streets, and I followed the dog recommendations of some friends. And as for some, I vouch never again to ask them for food advice. Some of the dog joints I was directed to visit served up rubber dogs, one place heated the dog up in the microwave (a felony, as I mentioned before), and outside one lovely place a skinny rat followed me back to my car. Perhaps he knew I would take one bite from that nasty dog and feel compelled to toss the remains onto the sidewalk. I may be a man of many unsavory traits, but my momma did not raise a litter bug. After taking two bites, I drove off to find a garbage can down the street to toss that tasteless dog into, and left that rat to stand there alone, still skinny, and ready to antagonize the next visitor to that unnamed eatery to which I shall never again return.

As a few of my jokester buddies suggested, maybe I knocked some time off of my lifeline by inhaling all of those dogs in such a short time. Hey, who the hell knows? My only goal on longevity at this point is to outlive my three-year-old mini Australian Shepherd, Rocky. I turn 60 this year so if I make it to 75, I figure I'll accomplish that goal. If not, Rocky wins the bet.

But through my love of the Chicago hot dog, I had the opportunity to meet some great people and to traverse the neighborhoods of the city I love—covering all points north, south, east and west. I felt like a Streets and San Man again, cruising through the different areas— observing the goings on at this corner, and the hustle happening in this city nook or that cranny. It was all good for the stomach, the soul, and the pen. So to you, the Chicago dog, I say THANKS for giving me the opportunity to get out and about again. It was a great ride.

Coupons on the Following Page

The bearer of this coupon is entitled to a discount of $1.00 with the purchase of $10.00 or more at (in store purchase only):

FAT TOMMY'S
$1.00 off

Expires 7-1-2021 – Coupon taken from the book, NO KETCHUP

The bearer of this coupon is entitled to a discount of $1.00 with the purchase of $10.00 or more at (in store purchase only):

SUSIE'S DRIVE In
$1.00 off

Expires 7-1-2021 – Coupon taken from the book, NO KETCHUP

The bearer of this coupon is entitled to a discount of $1.00 with the purchase of $10.00 or more at (in store purchase only):

THE LAUNCHING PAD
$1.00 off

Expires 7-1-2021 – Coupon taken from the book, NO KETCHUP

The bearer of this coupon is entitled to a discount of $1.00 with the purchase of $10.00 or more at (in store purchase only):

HENRY'S DRIVE IN
$1.00 off

Expires 7-1-2021 – Coupon taken from the book, NO KETCHUP

The bearer of this coupon is entitled to a discount of $1.00 with the purchase of $10.00 or more at (in store purchase only):

NICKY V's
$1.00 off

Expires 7-1-2021 – Coupon taken from the book, NO KETCHUP

The bearer of this coupon is entitled to a discount of $1.00 with the purchase of $10.00 or more at (in store purchase only):

CHUBBY WIENERS
$1.00 off

Expires 7-1-2021 – Coupon taken from the book, NO KETCHUP

The bearer of this coupon is entitled to a discount of $1.00 with the purchase of $10.00 or more at (in store purchase only):

THE DUCK INN & Duck Inn Dogs
$1.00 off

Expires 7-1-2021 – Coupon taken from the book, NO KETCHUP

NO KETCHUP – Chicago's Top 50 Hot Dogs

NO KETCHUP – Chicago's Top 50 Hot Dogs

NO KETCHUP – Chicago's Top 50 Hot Dogs

NO KETCHUP – Chicago's Top 50 Hot Dogs

NO KETCHUP – Chicago's Top 50 Hot Dogs

NO KETCHUP – Chicago's Top 50 Hot Dogs

NO KETCHUP – Chicago's Top 50 Hot Dogs

The bearer of this coupon is entitled to a discount of $1.00 with the
purchase of $10.00 or more at (in store purchase only):

FAT JOHNNIES
$1.00 off

Expires 7-1-2021 – Coupon taken from the book, NO KETCHUP

The bearer of this coupon is entitled to a discount of $1.00 with the
purchase of $10.00 or more at (in store purchase only):

BRANKO'S SANDWICH SHOP
$1.00 off

Expires 7-1-2021 – Coupon taken from the book, NO KETCHUP

The bearer of this coupon is entitled to a discount of $1.00 with the
purchase of $10.00 or more at (in store purchase only):

FATSO'S LAST STAND
$1.00 off

Expires 7-1-2021 – Coupon taken from the book, NO KETCHUP

The bearer of this coupon is entitled to a discount of $1.00 with the
purchase of $10.00 or more at (in store purchase only):

BYRON'S HOT DOGS
$1.00 off

Expires 7-1-2021 – Coupon taken from the book, NO KETCHUP

The bearer of this coupon is entitled to a discount of $1.00 with the
purchase of $10.00 or more at (in store purchase only):

CARM'S BEEF
$1.00 off

Expires 7-1-2021 – Coupon taken from the book, NO KETCHUP

The bearer of this coupon is entitled to a discount of $1.00 with the
purchase of $10.00 or more at (in store purchase only):

GEORGE'S GYROS
$1.00 off

Expires 7-1-2021 – Coupon taken from the book, NO KETCHUP

The bearer of this coupon is entitled to a discount of $1.00 with the
purchase of $10.00 or more at (in store purchase only):

LU LU's Hot Dogs
$1.00 off

Expires 7-1-2021 – Coupon taken from the book, NO KETCHUP

NO KETCHUP – Chicago's Top 50 Hot Dogs

NO KETCHUP – Chicago's Top 50 Hot Dogs

NO KETCHUP – Chicago's Top 50 Hot Dogs

NO KETCHUP – Chicago's Top 50 Hot Dogs

NO KETCHUP – Chicago's Top 50 Hot Dogs

NO KETCHUP – Chicago's Top 50 Hot Dogs

NO KETCHUP – Chicago's Top 50 Hot Dogs

HOT DOG STAND LOCATIONS

Downtown/and nearby

Carm's Beef 109
Dog House Grill 45
Fast Track 86
Express Grill 93-95
Jim's Original 93-95
Martin's Corner 50-51

North

Branko's Sandwich Shop 45-50, 67, 68
Byron's 68, 65-79, 110
Chicago's Dog House 103-104
Clark Street Dogs 101
Devil Dogs 101
Flub a Dub Chubs 80, 110
Hot G 58-59, 110
Jake's Pup in the Ruf 8, 68
Red Hot Ranch 15, 30
Wiener Circle 36, 68
Wrigleyville Dogs 45

Northwest

Budacki's Drive In 104-108, 110
Bob O's 87
Chubby Wieners 97-100, 110
Mr. D's Shish Kabob 29-30
Quick Bite 20
Susie's Drive In 15-19

Far Northwest

Wolfy's 14, 64-65, 110
The Plush Pup 108
Snappy Dog 41-42
Superdawg 35, 68, 110

South

Don's Drive In 5, 108, 110
Fat Johnnies 55-58, 68, 110

<u>INDEX</u>

<u>INDEX</u> (continued)

<u>INDEX</u> (continued)

About the Author

A life-long Chicagoan, Dennis Foley is the author of three books and two award-winning screenplays. Dennis' first book, *The Streets and San Man's Guide to Chicago Eats*, a handbook of Chicago's off-the-beaten-track eateries, won a Midwest Independent Publishers Association award (1st Place for humor). He also authored a memoir, *The Drunkard's Son*, and a novel, *The Blue Circus*, both set in Chicago. *No Ketchup* is his fourth book.

Dennis wrote the screenplay, *Not a Stranger,* which was filmed on Chicago's South Side in 2015. It received a 3-star review from film critic Richard Roeper upon its screening in 2016, and went on to be nominated for or win several awards on the film festival circuit, including—Top Screenplay (Golden Door Film Festival) and Top Debut Film (Route 66 Film Festival). The film has since received distribution and is now available on Amazon Prime and other outlets.

Married to his bride Susan for over thirty years, they have three sons—Matt-30, Pat-28, and Mike-20. He holds an MFA in Creative Writing from Columbia College-Chicago, and a JD from The John Marshall Law School. He is also a proud graduate of Christian Brothers University in Memphis. Over the years, Dennis has had the pleasure of working as a bouncer, assistant state's attorney, criminal defense attorney, dog-walker, electrician, beer-line cleaner, teacher, and coach. In addition to working on his craft, Dennis founded and runs a lacrosse program for South Side kids and still uses his legal skills on occasion to keep his friends out of jail.